Skyline 3

Student's Book

Simon Brewster

Paul Davies

Mickey Rogers

NO LONGER
PROPERTY OF PPLD

MACMILLAN

PIKES PEAK LIBRARY DISTRICT

16705338 8

Contents

Functions

- Talking about past events and experiences
- Talking about past habits
- Contrasting the past and the present

- Talking about present lifestyle and future plans
- Making comparisons
- Giving opinions

- Giving opinions
- Making predictions
- Talking about conditions and results
- Giving advice

- Giving opinions
- Talking about social customs
- Discussing and stating preferences

- Talking about fortune
- Talking about plans
- Talking about shopping
- Talking about inflation

- Talking about home entertainment
- Talking about places to visit
- Talking about likes, dislikes and preferences
- Talking about TV

Vocabulary

- Personal information
- so / too / either / neither
- Life events

- The family
- Participial adjectives – interested / interesting
- Leisure activities
- Cognates

- Types of energy sources
- The body and its functions
- Health and fitness

- Loan words
- Country and city life
- Problems of urbanization

- Collocations
- Money
- Shopping

- Movie vocabulary
- Television vocabulary

Pronunciation

- Sounds – past tense endings

- Contractions

- Sentences stress – first conditional

- Word stress

- Word stress

- Sounds – "o" as / ʌ / or / oʊ /

Contents

Functions

- Describing celebrations and customs
- Describing food
- Talking about customs in your own country
- Talking about cultural differences

- Talking about health and your body
- Making suggestions
- Expressing opinions
- Talking about possibilities

- Talking about wishes and dreams
- Talking about imaginary situations

- Giving opinions
- Talking about likes and dislikes
- Reporting what someone said
- Asking polite questions

- Talking about discoveries and inventions
- Talking about past plans that went wrong
- Describing things

- Giving reasons
- Guessing meaning from context
- Persuading
- Describing advertisements

Vocabulary

- Festivals
- Food and ingredients
- Culture

- Body parts
- Types of exercise
- Illnesses
- Symptoms
- Remedies

- Words with similar meanings
  – *wish* / *hope* / *expect* / *wait*

- Virtual reality
- Travel
- Tourism and the tourist industry

- Word formation
- Technology

- Clothing
- Advertising
- Collocation
- Synonyms

Pronunciation

- Weak forms – verb + *to*

- Word stress

- Sentence stress – second conditional

- Intonation – question forms

- Weak forms – *was* / *were*

- Review of numbers

Unit 1 Life stories

1 Personal history

1 Speaking

In groups, discuss what you know about the people in the photographs. Use words from the box to help you.

born	lived
married	divorced
studied	visited
died	worked

2 Reading and speaking

a Work in pairs. Student A, read about Princess Diana. Student B, read about Prince William.

b Student A, ask questions about Prince William to complete his profile.
Student B, ask questions about Princess Diana to complete her profile.

DIANA
A TROUBLED PRINCESS

Diana Spencer was born in Sandringham, England, in 1961. When she was 8 years old, her parents divorced. So, when she married royalty in 1981, at the age of 20, she wanted her marriage to be for life. By 1984 she was the mother of two sons, and her marriage seemed to be perfect. Unfortunately, her marriage was already in serious trouble. In 1992, she separated "temporarily" from her husband. Then in August 1996 the impossible happened. She got divorced. The people of Britain still loved their princess and there were always stories about her in the newspapers.

Everybody wanted her to be happy, so when she died in a car crash in Paris in August 1997, just one year after her divorce, the whole country went into mourning. She is buried at Althorp, her family home, and thousands of people visit her grave every year.

William: A Profile

Full name: ....
Date of birth: ....
Place of birth: ....
High school: ....
University: ....
Favorite sports: ....
Likes: ....

William

The Next Generation

Prince William (William Arthur Philip Louis Windsor) was born in London on June 21, 1982. When he was three years old, he began attending a pre-school in London. His parents wanted him to have a "normal" childhood and education. William was a good student, and when he was 13, he went to Eton College, where he received his high school education. He is now attending St. Andrews University in Scotland.

And what is the future King of England like? He is both a good student and an excellent athlete. He used to be captain of the swimming team at Eton, and now he plays polo, like his father. And, like most young people his age, he likes techno music and video games, and he has many friends. He has as normal a life as possible for a future king!

Diana: A Profile

Full name: ....
Date of birth: ....
Place of birth: ....
Date of marriage: ....
Date of divorce: ....
Date of death: ....
How she died: ....

3 Pronunciation: sounds – past tense endings

a   Listen to the pronunciation of these past tense verbs and write them in the appropriate column.

lived	worked	depended	divorced	separated	happened	stopped	wanted	married

formed /d/	crossed /t/	departed /ɪd/

b   Listen and check.

c   Practice saying the verbs.

4 Speaking and writing

a   In pairs, talk about your personal history. While your partner is talking, take notes. Ask questions for clarification or more information. Use William's profile for ideas.

When were you born?

b   Use your notes to write a short biography of your partner.

c   Exchange papers. Read your biography and correct any incorrect information.

2 Unforgettable memories

1 Listening and speaking

a This is a true story. Peter was a boy when it happened. In pairs, look at the photograph. What do you think his story is about?

b Now listen and answer the questions.

1 What was Peter doing when he saw the animal?
2 What was it?
3 What was his first reaction?
4 What did he do next?
5 What was the animal doing when the police arrived?

c In pairs, discuss what happened.

2 Grammar builder: review of past progressive vs. past simple

a Match the sentences with the timelines.

A — was calling his father — saw the robber — Present

B — called his father — saw the robber — Present

1 Sam called his father when he saw the robber.
2 Sam was calling his father when he saw the robber.

b Complete this article with correct forms of the verbs in parentheses.

PETER AND THE BIG CAT

Twelve-year-old Peter Sutton had the experience of his life yesterday. He was alone in the house, and he (1)............(*wash*) the dishes in the kitchen when he (2)............(*see*) a large animal in the yard. At first, he (3)............(*think*) it was a big dog. When he (4)............(*realize*) the animal was a tiger, he (5)............(*feel*) very frightened. He (6)............(*shake*) all over, he said, but he (7)............(*go*) to the kitchen door and (8)............(*shut*) it. He then (9)............(*call*) the police. When the police and a tiger trainer (10)............(*arrive*), the tired young Bengal tiger (11)............(*sleep*) peacefully in the sun outside the kitchen door. Peter (12)............(*look*) down at it from the window of his bedroom upstairs, with the door locked. What a story to tell at school!

3 Writing and speaking

a Write a paragraph about an interesting experience in your life. Use the questions in the box to help you.

When and where did it happen?	**What were you doing at the time?**
What did you do? / How did you react?	**How did the experience end?**

b Now tell your group or class your story.

4 Word builder: *so / too / either / neither*

a Look at the examples.

1 *A:* *I have a new car.*
   B: *I do* **too!** */ So do I!*

2 *A:* *I liked the movie.*
   B: *I did* **too.** */ So did I.*

3 *A:* *Joe doesn't work full time.*
   B: *Carl doesn't* **either**. */* **Neither** *does Carl.*

4 *A:* *Marsha didn't go to the party.*
   B: *I didn't* **either**. */* **Neither** *did I.*

What are *so, too, either* and *neither* used to express?

a) similarity   **b)** difference   **c)** surprise

b Mary and Sean are at a party. Complete their conversation using *so, too, either* or *neither*.

Mary: Hello. My name's Mary. I'm from Ireland.

Sean: Ah, (1)......................... am I! I'm Sean. Where are you from in Ireland?

Mary: Well, I was born in Cork.

Sean: Really! I was (2).......................... . Did you go to UCC?

Mary: No, I didn't go to university.

Sean: (3)......................... did I. I went to Cork Technical College.

Mary: Ah! So did I. But I didn't graduate there, I'm afraid.

Sean: Really? I didn't (4)......................... .

Mary: It was terrible. They said I was copying, but someone was copying from *me*. Hey – your name's Sean, you say? Sean Murphy? It was you!

Sean: No, I'm Sean ... uh ... Reilly. Oh dear! It's eight o'clock. I have to go. Bye!

Language assistant		
subject + auxiliary / *be* + **too / either**		
I	do	**too**.
I	don't	**either**.
So / Neither + auxiliary / *be* + subject		
Neither	is	she.
So	do	I.

5 Speaking

a Check (✓) the things in the table that are true for you.

	✓	NAME		✓	NAME
I was born in a small town.			I wasn't born in a small town.		
I'm an only child.			I'm not an only child.		
I liked sports at school.			I didn't like sports at school.		
I use the Internet a lot.			I don't use the Internet at all.		

b Now find someone with three or more things the same as you. Write the other student's name beside each thing under *Name*.

A: *I was born in a small town.*
B: *So was I. I'm not an only child.*
A: *Neither am I. I ...*

3 Now and then

1 Speaking and reading

a Look at the photograph of two men. What do you think they do?

b Read the article and match the topics with the paragraphs.

1 Preparing to start a business ...

2 The business today ...

3 The early days of the business ...

4 Ben and Jerry's school days ...

From Hippies to Millionaires

1

Ben and Jerry didn't like school. They weren't interested in math, science or English, and they didn't use to study very much. They preferred listening to music, going out with girls and eating good food.

2

When Ben and Jerry finished high school, they didn't want to go to college. They wanted to work, but most of all, they wanted to have fun. Their first idea was to start a bagel business, but the equipment cost $40,000! Then they decided to take an ice cream making course, which cost $5.00 each, a more reasonable price. They bought some cheap equipment, and they used to spend hours making ice cream.

3

In 1978, Ben and Jerry made ice cream their business. They moved to Burlington, Vermont and opened Ben and Jerry's Homemade Ice Cream Parlor. This was not an ordinary ice cream parlor. The ice cream flavors had crazy names like Chunky Monkey and Totally Nuts. The parlor offered jugglers and live music. And the ice cream was delicious!

4

Soon Ben and Jerry were distributing ice cream to stores and restaurants in Burlington. Their ice cream became more and more popular, and today there are thousands of Ben and Jerry's outlets all over the world. The guys who used to be the school's "bad boys" are now millionaires. But the ice cream still has crazy names, and it's still delicious. Some things don't change!

c In pairs, discuss these questions.

1 What were Ben and Jerry like when they were in school?

2 Why did they choose ice cream as their business?

3 Why was their first ice cream parlor a success?

4 How is Ben and Jerry's business different today?

5 How is their business the same?

2 Grammar builder: *used to*

a Look at these examples.

*What did Ben and Jerry **use to** do in high school?*
*They **used to** be hippies.   They **didn't use to** study very much.*

What does *used to* express?

a) An action in progress at a specific time in the past.   **b)** A state or habitual action in the past.

b Find two more examples of *used to* in the article about Ben and Jerry.
How do you express *used to* in your language?

3 Listening and speaking

a Look at the pictures and listen to the conversation. Write *past* and *present* under the appropriate picture.

b Listen again and check (✓) the things Andy used to do.

1	have long hair	○
2	work in an office	○
3	ride a motorcycle to work	○
4	work six to seven hours	○
5	not like working	○
6	have short hair	○
7	repair motorcycles	○
8	drive a car to work	○
9	work ten hours	○
10	love working	○

c In pairs, check your answers.
   A: Did Andy use to have long hair?
   B: No, he didn't. He used to have short hair, and he didn't use to have a mustache.

4 Writing and speaking

a Write three or four sentences about differences in your life today and in the past. Don't write your name.
   I used to live in an apartment, but now I live in a house. I didn't use to want children,
   but now I want a lot of children!

b In groups, mix up the papers. Take a paper and read the sentences. The group
tries to guess who wrote them.

4 Lifeline to scholarships and jobs

1 Reading, writing and speaking

a Complete this questionnaire.

USE OF ENGLISH *check (✓) as appropriate*

Do you use English in your study / work at present?   *Yes, a lot* ☐   *Yes, a little* ☐   *No* ☐

If yes, what do you use it for?   *Reading* ☐   *Correspondence* ☐   *Telephoning* ☐   *Other:* _____

Are you probably going to use
English in your future study / work?   *Yes, definitely* ☐   *Yes, probably* ☐   *Yes, possibly* ☐   *No* ☐

Is an application / interview in English a possibility in your future?   *Yes* ☐   *No* ☐

If yes, will it probably be for: *study or training* ☐   *a scholarship* ☐   *a job* ☐   *a promotion* ☐

---

b In groups, discuss your answers to the questionnaire. Then report to the class and answer these questions.

1 Who in your group uses English most at present? What for?

2 Who in your group will probably use English most in the future? What for?

3 How important will English be in your future?

2 Reading

a Look at the title of the advertisement on page 13.

Circle the words and phrases you expect to see.

| course | soccer | expenses | photograph | interview | résumé |
| study | career | fee | college degree | research | computer |

b Read the advertisement and check your answers.

c Read these statements about the advertisement. Are they T (true) or F (false)?

1 This is a very basic course in solar energy.   T ○   F ○

2 Students have to find somewhere to live.   T ○   F ○

3 The scholarships are not for U.S. citizens.   T ○   F ○

4 The scholarships cover all the candidates' expenses.   T ○   F ○

5 Résumés should be short.   T ○   F ○

6 The selection process includes an interview.   T ○   F ○

SCHOLARSHIPS FOR SOLAR ENERGY COURSE

Three scholarships available for:
one-month advanced course in solar energy systems on:

- latest available technology
- maintenance and improvement
- research and developments in progress

Scholarships include:

- economy air fare
- course fee
- accommodations in a student residence
- three basic meals per day

No other expenses included.

Requirements:

- relevant college degree
- at least two years' experience in the area of solar energy
- age 25 to 45
- non-U.S. citizenship
- good level of English

If you are interested, send a brief, relevant résumé, a brief letter explaining why you are an appropriate candidate for a scholarship and a recent photograph to Jack Leng at the address below. U.S. Consular staff will interview selected candidates in their country.

3 Reading and speaking

a Read the résumé for the scholarship.

R É S U M É

NAME:	*Daniel Romeu*
DATE OF BIRTH:	*October 21, 1971*
NATIONALITY:	*Nicaraguan*
PLACE OF RESIDENCE:	*Managua, Nicaragua*

QUALIFICATIONS:

- High school diploma (1986)
- Degree in Mechanical Engineering, Universidad Americana (1993)
- Certificate, two-month course in solar heating (1996)
- English level: intermediate

WORK EXPERIENCE:

- Production Assistant involved in production of solar panels, Soltec, S.A. (1996-1998)
- Production Manager in charge of textile quality, Industria Textil Colón (1999)

b In groups, discuss the weak points and strong points of the candidate. Use the ideas in the box to help you.

professional training and qualifications	work experience
command of English	**presentation of the résumé**

c Would you accept the candidate? Why or why not? Take a class vote.

Unit 2　Work and play

1 Modern careers

1 Speaking and reading

a Look at the pictures.
What do you think the article is going to be about?

b Read the article and complete the timeline.

KEEPING IN TOUCH

Jake Wilkins was born in 1907 and his wife Rachel in 1912, both in Wisconsin. Jake worked all his life on the family farm, like his father and grandfather. Rachel helped on the farm, but mostly took care of the house and the children. In those days, most boys went into the same work as their fathers, and few went to college. Most girls didn't even think of higher education and a career.

Jake and Rachel's son, Bobby, was the first in the Wilkins family to attend college. He graduated in 1955, when he was 22, not in agriculture, but in chemistry. Like many boys of his generation, he broke with tradition and chose his own career. He married Cindy, daughter of the local store keeper, six years later and they settled in Racine, Wisconsin, not far from their parents. He worked in a pharmaceutical company, and she worked as a secretary. Bobby was still working for the same

pharmaceutical company when he retired at age 60.

In their late thirties, Cindy and Bobby had a daughter, Andrea. After majoring in communication technology, she worked in Chicago for a few years, moved to New York to do a Master's, then to California, where she has worked since 1998. She's now doing a doctorate part-time and spends a lot of time at conventions and seminars, keeping up with developments.

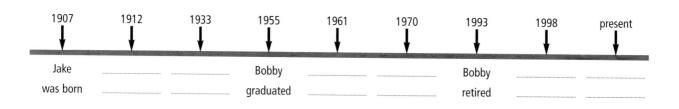

1907	1912	1933	1955	1961	1970	1993	1998	present
Jake was born			Bobby graduated			Bobby retired		

c   **In groups, discuss these questions.**

1   Andrea is the youngest member of the Wilkins family. How will the family history continue?

2   What do you think Andrea will probably do?

I think she'll probably ... / She might ... / I imagine she's going to ...

2 Listening

a   **Listen to the conversation.**

1   Who is Andrea talking to?

2   What are they talking about?

b   **Listen again. Complete the notes about Andrea's plans. Did you guess the family's future correctly?**

1   In December, she's going to ....

2   In April, ...

3   In June, ...

4   In July, ...

5   In about three years, ...

3 Writing and speaking

a   **Write a paragraph about your family. Use the ideas in the box to help you.**

What kind of education did your grandparents and parents have?	Did the women work only in the home?	Did the men do the same work as their fathers?	How many children did they have?
What are you doing now?	Are you married, or do you plan to get married?	Would you like to have children? How many?	Do you want your children to live in the same city as you and work in the same job as you?

b   **In groups, use the information in your paragraph to talk about your family.**

2 Living to work, or working to live?

1 Reading and speaking

a In groups, discuss these questions.

1 What is a workaholic?

2 Do you know any workaholics?

b Read and answer the quiz.

Are you a Workaholic? *Take this quiz to find out! Answer each question truthfully.*

1 Is your work more exciting than activities with your family or anything else?

2 Do you take work home with you?

3 Is work the activity you like to do best and talk about most?

4 Do you get impatient with people who have other priorities apart from work?

5 Do you do things energetically and competitively, including play?

6 Are you irritated when people ask you to stop working in order to do something else?

7 Do you think about your work while driving, falling asleep or when others are talking?

8 Do you work or read during meals?

7-8 "yes" answers - you really are a workaholic. Slow down! Don't live to work.

5-6 "yes" answers - you think about work too much.

3-4 "yes" answers - you have a good balance between work and free time.

1-2 "yes" answers - you work enough, but you don't work too much.

0 "yes" answers - you are definitely not a workaholic! You work to live.

c In groups, discuss who you think is a workaholic in the group. Then compare quiz results and see if you were right.

2 Word builder: participial adjectives

a Look at these rules. Then complete the sentences with *interested* or *interesting*.

Use the past participle to indicate how you feel about something: *I'm interested in sports.*
Use the present participle to describe something: *Basketball is interesting.*

1 We offered him the job, but he wasn't ....

2 I think that's a very .... idea.

3 She's a very .... person. I have to confess I'm .... in her.

4 **A:** Good morning. Can I help you?

B: Yes, I'm .... in a swimsuit.

b Use the correct form of the verbs in the box to write sentences about your opinions of these topics.

baseball   romantic movies   soccer   soap operas   horror movies

bore	excite	embarrass	interest	frighten

I get very excited about baseball – it's a very interesting game.

3 **Grammar builder:** review of *might / will / going to*

a Look at these sentences from the conversation in lesson 1.

He'll take care of the house and work on his book.
We're going to move to Boston in July.
We might have a child in about three years.

1 Which two sentences refer to plans in the future?

2 Which sentence refers to a possibility in the future?

b Write answers for these questions.

1 What are you doing after class today?

2 What are you going to do when this course finishes?

3 Your friend needs to pass an important English exam for a job. What will you do to help?

4 Where will you probably live after you retire?

Language assistant

Use *going to* or present progressive for plans or arrangements:

*I'm **going to** study tonight.*
*I'm **studying** tonight.*

Going to often indicates intention. The present progressive often indicates a more fixed arrangement (like marriage).

*I'm **going to get married** in June.*
*I'm **getting married** in June.*

Use *will* for offers and for things you expect to happen in the future:

I'll help you with your project.
I'll (probably) live at home after I graduate.

---

4 **Pronunciation:** contractions

a We normally use contractions (e.g. *I'm*) when we speak. Listen to the sentences. Check (✔) the sentence you hear.

1 **a)** We're going to study tomorrow night. ◯

b) We are going to study tomorrow night. ◯

2 **a)** I'll call you tomorrow. ◯

b) I will call you tomorrow. ◯

3 **a)** He's leaving for New York tomorrow. ◯

b) He is leaving for New York tomorrow. ◯

b In pairs, practice saying the sentences.

5 **Speaking**

In groups, talk about ways to improve the quality of your life.

A: *I'm sort of a workaholic. I'm going to take more vacations and spend more time with my friends and family.*

B: *I don't like my job very much, and I'm interested in photography. I'll probably take some classes because I'd like to work as a photographer some day.*

17

3

Relaxation and play

1 Speaking

a Look at the photographs. Decide which three activities are the best for relaxing.

b In groups, discuss your opinions.
Use the expressions in the box to help you.

> *A: I think running is relaxing because*
> *when you exercise, you have less stress.*
>
> *B: But running can be dangerous!*

I think ...	**I agree. And I think ...**

I don't agree.
In my opinion, ... is more relaxing than ...

boring	**interesting**
exciting	**dangerous**

stressful

A
cooking

B
running

C
gardening

D
doing yoga

E
playing computer games

F
skydiving

2 Grammar builder: review of comparatives and superlatives

a Look at the examples. Then complete the table with correct forms of the adjectives in the box.

1 *Mark is **richer than** Joe, but Sam is **the richest** of the three.*
2 *A: I think Boston is **more beautiful than** San Francisco.*
  *B: I don't agree. San Francisco is **the most beautiful city** I've ever seen.*

stressful	interesting	pretty	nice	dirty	hot	relaxing	cheap	funny

-er than	the -est	more ... than	the most ...
nicer than	the nicest		

b Complete the conversation with the correct form of the adjectives in parentheses.

Carl: I need a break. I want to do something fun!

Dennis: OK. What's (1) ....(*exciting*) thing to do in the world?

Carl: I don't know. What?

Dennis: Skydiving, of course!

Carl: Are you serious? I think that's (2) ....(*dangerous*) thing to do in the world
– even (3) ....(*dangerous*) than hang gliding!

Dennis: But it's also a lot (4) ....(*exciting*) than hang gliding.

Carl: Well, it's not exactly (5) ....(*cheap*) sport in the world, either, Dennis.

Dennis: Oh, come on. One afternoon of skydiving is (6) ....(*cheap*) than going out of town
for the weekend.

Carl: Dennis, you're (7) ....(*crazy*) person I know. I'd rather go out of town than jump
out of an airplane!

3 Listening

a Carl is making plans for the weekend. Listen to the conversation. What are they going to do?

b Listen again and mark the sentences T (true) or F (false).

1 Carl likes antique cars.   T ◯   F ◯

2 Dennis doesn't want to go to the beach.   T ◯   F ◯

3 Dennis wants to go out with Carla Miller.   T ◯   F ◯

4 The baseball game on Sunday is an important game.   T ◯   F ◯

5 Tom and Dennis think a party is a good idea.   T ◯   F ◯

6 Dennis's house is the worst place for a party.   T ◯   F ◯

7 They're probably going to invite Carla Miller.   T ◯   F ◯

4 Speaking

a In pairs, agree on the following things.

1 the most relaxing activity
2 the most exciting sport
3 the best place for a vacation in your country
4 the prettiest city in your country

5 a more dangerous sport than skydiving
6 a faster way of communicating than e-mail
7 the best way to learn English
8 the most boring weekend activity

b Work with another pair. Try to guess their opinions. You can have three guesses for each category.
Give three points for a correct first guess, two points for a correct second guess and one point for a
correct third guess.

Pair 1: *For you, the most relaxing activity is reading.*   *Pair 1*: *Is it sleeping?*

Pair 2: *Wrong!*   *Pair 2*: *That's right. Two points.*

4 Lifeline to psychology

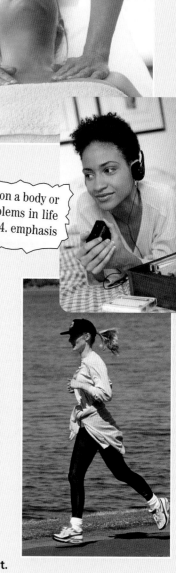

1 Reading and speaking

Read the dictionary definitions of *stress*.
Then, in pairs, discuss which definition is related to:

1 linguistics ....

2 physics / engineering ....

3 psychology ....

4 and which is general ....

stress /stres/ *n.* 1. effect of a force or weight upon a body or structure 2. tension or anxiety caused by problems in life 3. emphasis or importance given to something 4. emphasis or accentuation of syllables in speech

How do you express each of these ideas of stress in your native language?

2 Word builder: cognates

a Look at these words from the article on page 21. How many do you recognize?

phenomenon	urgent	defend	crucial	constant	adrenaline
pupils	dilate	vision	profound	oxygen	glucose	digestion
constant	accumulate	toxic	intestines	vulnerable	circulatory

b Why do you recognize them?

3 Reading and speaking

a In pairs, discuss the statements below. In your opinion, are they true?
Under "Your opinion," put a check (✓) (true) or an (✗) (false) for each statement.

	Your opinion	The article
1 Stress is normal in animals.		
2 Stress can improve physical abilities and strength.		
3 Stress immediately interferes with thinking and memory.		
4 Stress accelerates the digestive process.		
5 Stress reduces defenses against infection.		
6 Stress eliminates toxins from the body.		
7 Stress can cause stomach ulcers.		
8 Stress can cause circulatory problems.		

b Now read the article and put (✓) or (✗) for each statement under "The article."
Compare your opinion and the article.

THE PURPOSE AND EFFECTS OF STRESS

Stress is a frequent phenomenon in animals. It is a response to urgent needs or danger, and often allows animals to survive by obtaining food, defending themselves, or escaping. In the African Savannah, the tense lions and the nervous gazelles are both feeling stress prior to crucial action.

Humans once lived in the same world of basic needs and dangers as animals. Today, we do not usually have to hunt for food, physically defend ourselves or escape, but we still face constant stressful challenges. We create many of them in our minds: the worry of failing an exam, the challenge of getting good grades.

In tense situations – in the wilds of Africa or in a Manhattan office – stress causes the release of adrenaline into the blood. The pupils of the eyes dilate for better vision, breathing is more profound, and the heart beats faster to send more oxygen and glucose to the muscles and brain. Digestion stops, memory and thinking become sharper, and the body becomes stronger, ready to respond.

When the body has time to recover from stress, there is no problem. But when the stress is constant,

problems can accumulate. During periods of stress, the immune system weakens and there is a greater risk of infection. Adrenaline is toxic in large quantities and arrested digestion leaves the stomach and intestines vulnerable to ulcers. Increased blood pressure damages the circulatory system. Some stress can produce a better performance, but constant stress can damage the body, and eventually kill.

c In groups, discuss these questions about stress in animals and human beings.

1 Why don't wild animals normally suffer from stress-related health problems?

2 Why do human beings often suffer from these problems?

3 What are some of the physical problems associated with high levels of stress?

4 Why are human stress problems probably more common now than in the past?

4 Writing, reading and speaking

a Write a short paragraph about the presence of stress in your life. Use the questions in the box to help you.

Do you suffer from stress?
If not, why not?
If so, what are some causes of stress in your life?

b Exchange paragraphs with a partner. Read your partner's paragraph and write recommendation for lowering his/her stress. Use the photographs on pages 20 and 21 to help you.

c Exchange papers again. In pairs, read and discuss the recommendations.

1 Check your progress

got	met	took	was
went	were working	when
used to	younger	youngest

a Read the biography. Complete it using words or phrases from the box.

Biography

Nicole Kidman was born in Hawaii in 1967, but her family (1) .... back to Australia when she was four years old. Her parents had strong opinions about almost everything. Every day (2) .... start with physical exercises for Nicole and her (3) .... sister. At meals, the conversation was usually political. As a girl, Nicole loved ballet, and she (4) .... classes in dance and drama.

She (5) .... a striking teenager – very tall, with pale skin and red hair. Soon she was one of the (6) .... actresses at Sydney's Philip Street Theater. She (7) .... her first big acting opportunity as a 16-year-old in the Australian television movie *Bush Christmas*. She made her first American movie in 1989. In the same year, Nicole (8) .... Tom Cruise (9) .... the two of them (10) .... in *Days of Thunder*. They married in 1990.

b Choose the correct word to complete the conversation.

A: Nicole Kidman was born in the U.S., wasn't she?

B: Yes, and (11) *either / neither / so / too* was Mel Gibson.

A: Yeah, but he didn't (12) *go / going / was / went* to Australia until he was 12 years old.

B: I think his *Mad Max* movies are great.

A: Yes, I (13) *am / do / did / think* too. I didn't (14) *use / use to / used / used to* like that kind of movie, but *Mad Max* is special.

B: I (15) *was watching / watched* my video of *Mad Max II* when you (16) *called / were calling* me last night! I haven't decided yet, but I (17) *am going to / might / will* do my thesis on *Mad Max* movies.

A: Oh, yes – you're studying cinematography!

B: That's right. Hey, what (18) *are you doing / do you do / will you do* tonight? Let's watch *Mad Max III*.

A: Sure! That will be (19) *best / better / good* than watching TV.

B: Yes. And the (20) *best / more / most* useful thing for me will be your answers to my questionnaire.

A: Questionnaire? Ah, research for your thesis, I suppose.

Score out of 20

| ◯ 18–20 Excellent! | ◯ 15–17 Very good! | ◯ 12–14 OK, but review. | ◯ 9–11 You have some problems. Review units 1 and 2. | ◯ 0–8 Talk to your teacher. |

2 Games to play

a In teams, find ten adjectives in the word square.

b Then write five comparative or superlative sentences using the adjectives. The first team to get five correct sentences wins.

New York is the biggest city in the U.S.
Reading is more relaxing than running.

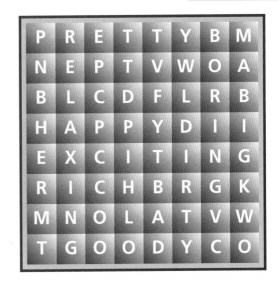

P	R	E	T	T	Y	B	M
N	E	P	T	V	W	O	A
B	L	C	D	F	L	R	B
H	A	P	P	Y	D	I	I
E	X	C	I	T	I	N	G
R	I	C	H	B	R	G	K
M	N	O	L	A	T	V	W
T	G	O	O	D	Y	C	O

3 Your world

a Complete the table about you.

	At age 10	Now
Getting up time:		
Going to bed time:		
Main daily activities:		
Hobbies or interests:		
Typical clothes:		
Best friends:		

b In pairs, discuss your answers.

A: I used to get up at 7 o'clock. I get up earlier now, usually at 6 o'clock. What about you?
B: I get up at the same time, six-thirty. But I go to bed much later than I used to.

4 Personal word bank

a Which of the adjectives in the box describe people (P) and which describe an event (E)? Which can describe both?

bored	boring	embarrassing	embarrassed ....
exciting	excited	interested	interesting ....
relaxing	relaxed	frightened	frightening ....

When an event is ...., people are ....

b But people as well as events can also have an effect on other people.

When a person is ...., other people are ....

Unit 3 Toward the future

1 Energy sources

1 Reading and speaking

a In groups, discuss these questions.

1 What things do we use energy for every day? (electric lights, computers, …)
2 How many energy sources can you name? (fossil fuels, …)
3 Which ones are renewable?

b Read and match the types of energy with the descriptions.

| geothermal | solar | nuclear | fossil fuels | hydroelectric | wind |

1 In this process, giant windmills are installed, usually on hills or mountains. When the wind blows, the blades of the windmills turn. This operates generators which make electricity. ....wind.....

Large panels, called photovoltaic cells (PV cells) are installed on walls or roofs of buildings. When the sun shines on the cells, they convert sunlight into electricity. **2**

3 If there are reserves of hot water below the surface of the earth, the water can be pumped to the surface to heat buildings. These reserves sometimes have large amounts of steam, which is used to turn turbines to create electricity. ....

This energy source comes from decayed plant and animal matter below the surface of the earth. Millions of years ago, the heat and pressure of the earth changed the organic matter into oil, natural gas and coal. **4**

Where there are fast flowing rivers, the water is used to turn giant turbines. The turbines are attached to generators which produce electricity. This type of energy can also come from ocean waves. **5**

Large amounts of energy are produced when atoms are split apart in a process called fission. This process creates heat, which heats water to operate steam turbines. The turbines produce electricity. **4**

c In groups, discuss these questions.

1 Which of the energy sources mentioned in the descriptions are most common in the world?
2 Which of the energy sources are most common in your country?
3 Which of the energy sources cause environmental problems?
4 Which are the most environmentally "friendly"?

2 Listening

a Listen to the first part of the interview. Which energy sources does the expert favor? Why?

b Listen to the second part of the interview. Why doesn't Dr. Allen favor the other two energy sources?

1 .... energy is .... and it isn't ....

2 .... energy is .... and it can be ....

3 Speaking and writing

a In pairs, complete the energy sources survey for your country.

ENERGY SOURCES SURVEY   Country ....   Region ....

Climate

1 a) rainy all year ☐   b) alternates between rainy and dry seasons ☐   c) dry all year ☐

2 a) usually windy ☐   b) windy certain times of the year ☐   c) almost never windy ☐

3 a) usually sunny ☐   b) alternates between sunny and cloudy ☐   c) usually cloudy ☐

Geography

a) plains or mountains ☐   b) coast ☐   c) rivers and streams ☐

d) geothermal areas ☐   e) limestone layers or salt domes (sources of fossil fuels) ☐

Energy sources currently in use in your country

a) fossil fuels ☐   b) nuclear ☐   c) geothermal ☐   d) hydroelectric ☐

e) solar ☐   f) wind ☐

Is your country an oil-producing country?

a) yes ☐   b) no ☐

---

b In groups, compare your answers to the survey. Discuss these questions.

1 What are the most common energy sources in your region?

2 Look at the answers to the survey. In your opinion, are alternative energy sources an option for your region? If so, which ones?

3 If there are already alternative sources in use, are they used by many people? If not, why not?

c With a partner, complete this short report on the energy situation in your region.

Report on Energy for the ... region of ...

The climate in the ... region is ...

The main geographical and geological characteristics are ...

The main energy sources in the region are currently ...

We recommend ... and ... as additional energy sources because ...

2 Predicting the future

A future car

C videobook

D e-book

B robot cleaner

1 Speaking

In groups, look at the photographs and discuss the objects.

1 Which ones exist now? Have you ever seen any of them?
2 Which ones do you think might exist in the future?
3 Which ones would you like to have? Why?

2 Reading and speaking

a Read these predictions made in the 20th century. Were they correct? Why or why not?

"The radio craze will die out in time." THOMAS EDISON, 1922

"While theoretically and technically television may be feasible, commercially and financially
I consider it an impossibility." LEE DEFOREST, INVENTOR OF THE AUDION TUBE (USED IN EARLY TELEVISIONS), 1926

"I think there is a world market for about five computers." THOMAS WATSON, CHAIRMAN OF IBM, 1943

"640K (of memory) should be enough for anybody." BILL GATES, 1981

"All the computers in the world will crash at 00:00 hours on January 1, 2000." THE MEDIA, 1999

b Now read some predictions about the 21st century and talk about them with a group.
Do you think any of them will be true?

I don't think people will have hovercrafts. I think they'll drive mini-cars.

WE ALL LIKE TO MAKE PREDICTIONS ABOUT THE FUTURE, BUT HOW OFTEN ARE OUR PREDICTIONS CORRECT?

Energy	There won't be any more fossil fuels. We will get all of our energy from the sun.
Transportation	People won't drive cars. Everyone will have a hovercraft.
Travel	The main tourist destinations will be recreation centers in space and on other planets.
Communications	People will send visual e-mail with video links. Computers won't be necessary for sending e-mails.
Shopping	There won't be stores. People will do their shopping on the Internet and it will be delivered to their houses.

c Make other predictions for the future.

I think Europe will become one big country.

3 Grammar builder: *will / won't* and *going to* for predictions

a **Look at these predictions.**

*People **will do** their shopping on the Internet.*
*Look at that boy in the tree – he's **going to fall**!*

1 Which one is more immediate and based on clear evidence?
2 Which one is more speculative?
3 Which verb form is used in each?

> **Language assistant**
>
> You can normally use **will / won't** for predictions instead of **going to**, but you cannot normally use **will / won't** for immediate predictions based on evidence.

b **Complete the conversation with the *will / won't* or *going to* form of the verbs in parentheses. Use *going to* only when necessary.**

Laura: Marilu is getting fat, isn't she?

Susan: No, she's not fat! She (1) .... (*have*) another baby.

Laura: Oh, how exciting!

Susan: Do you think you (2) .... (*have*) children?

Laura: No way! In five years I (3) .... (*be*) a famous fashion designer in New York.

Susan: Well, I (4) .... (*not have*) children in five years – but maybe later.

Laura: Hey, look at those clouds. It (5) .... (*rain*). Let's go!

4 Writing and speaking

a **Write a short paragraph making predictions about your life in five years. Use the questions in the box to help you.**

Where will you be?	Will you still be a student?

What kind of transportation will you have?

Will you be married?	If so, will you have children?

I think I will be in another country, probably Australia.
I won't be in a big city but probably on the coast.
I won't be a student – I'll probably be a teacher or a translator. I'll have a BMW and ...

b **In groups, compare your paragraphs. Ask for more information if you want to.**

A: Why Australia?

B: Because I like kangaroos.

C: Will you be rich?

B: Of course!

3 What if ...?

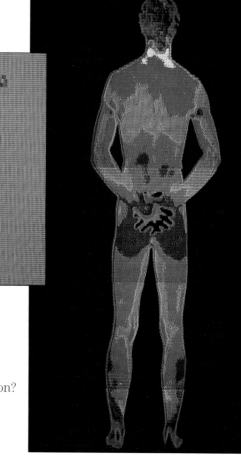

1 Listening

a Look at the list of activities and decide which use the most and the least energy.

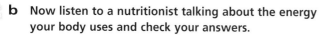

digesting food   body functions   physical activity

b Now listen to a nutritionist talking about the energy your body uses and check your answers.

c Listen again and answer the questions.

1   What percentage of energy is used for
   a) body functions?   **b)** physical activity?   **c)** eating and digestion?

2   Where does our energy come from?

2 Speaking and reading

a In pairs, number these activities in order from the most energetic (1) to the least energetic (8).

doing housework ....   swimming ....   playing soccer ....   playing basketball ....

watching TV ....   dancing ....   running ....   doing aerobics ....

b Read the article and check your answers.

CALORIES AND EXERCISE

Every type of exercise burns calories, but the number of calories burned will vary slightly based on your weight, body composition and the intensity of the exercise.

BASKETBALL – 576 calories an hour

Men and women need different amounts of calories: the average per day for men is 2,500 and for women 2,000. Your body burns calories all day, even when you aren't exercising. Team sports are often very energetic: in a basketball game you burn approximately 576 calories an hour, but in soccer it's only 504. Swimming for leisure burns about 460. You won't lose too much weight if you like disco dancing as this activity burns fewer calories an hour than swimming: 396. High impact aerobics uses a lot

of calories per hour: 720. Housework burns around 190 calories an hour. Watching TV burns only 81 calories an hour; sleeping burns 45.
What are the best activities for burning calories? Running and cycling very fast (1,188 calories burned per hour)!

SLEEPING – 45 calories an hour

Calculate your own calorie needs
If you want to calculate how many calories you need a day, you can use this formula:
Your weight in kilos x 38 = estimated calories per day, for example: 79 kilos x 38 = 3,002 calories.

3 Grammar builder: the first conditional

a Look at this example. Then answer the questions.

If you burn more calories than you eat, *you will lose* weight.

1 What does the clause with *if* refer to?

   a) a cause   **b)** an effect

2 What does the clause with *will / won't* refer to?

   a) a cause   **b)** an effect

> **Language assistant:**
> **word order in conditionals**
> The clause with *if* can go at the beginning or the end of the sentence:
> *If you eat too much, you won't lose weight.*
> *You won't lose weight if you eat too much.*

b Now use these phrases to write sentences with *if*.

Sally / be late – not / hurry up. ..Sally will be late if she doesn't hurry up...............................

1 We / not / buy tickets – miss the concert. ....

2 You / eat that cake – not / eat lunch. ....

3 James / be unhappy – Susan / not / go to the party. ....

4 We / not / go to the game – it / rain. ....

4 Pronunciation: sentence stress – first conditional

a Listen and underline the stressed words. Note that important words are stressed. Negatives are also stressed.

1 If you <u>don't</u> get up <u>early</u>, you'll be <u>late</u> for <u>work</u>.

2 You'll be fit if you exercise.

3 I'll call you if I can go to the party.

4 We won't arrive on time if we don't leave now.

b Listen again and practice the sentences.

5 Speaking

In teams, listen to your teacher read the first part of a sentence. Complete it logically and grammatically.

If you don't eat, ... you'll get very thin.

I'll be really happy if ... the school football team wins on Saturday.

Sentences

If you don't eat, ...   If Paul wins the lottery, ...

Mary will be late for class if ...   If I learn to speak English well, ...

If I don't study, ...   My teacher will give me a good grade if ...

If I get a new job, ...   If I go out tomorrow night, ...

We'll play soccer tomorrow if ...   My friends will think I'm crazy if ...

I won't come to class tomorrow if ...   I'll be really happy if ...

If you don't eat...   ...you'll get very thin.

4 Lifeline to health sciences

1 Speaking

a Are you fit for the future? How much do you know about health, diet and fitness? In pairs, mark the sentences T (true) or F (false).

b Discuss the answers with another pair. If possible, give reasons for your answers.

Health, Diet and Fitness Quiz

		T	F
1	You should eat at least six servings of carbohydrates per day (rice, cereals, beans, etc.).	○	○
2	You should drink six to eight glasses of water every day.	○	○
3	If you want to lose weight, you shouldn't eat any fat.	○	○
4	If you want to lose weight, never eat snacks between meals.	○	○
5	You won't lose weight if you eat too little.	○	○
6	For fitness, you need to exercise for at least an hour four times a week.	○	○
7	Being underweight is bad for your heart and brain.	○	○
8	Bone fractures are most common in overweight people.	○	○

2 Reading

Read the article and check your answers to the quiz in exercise **1**.
Underline the sentences where you find the answers.

Answers and Explanations about Health and Fitness

1 Carbohydrates are the body's main source of energy, and they should account for at least half of your daily calories. Try to eat six servings of foods like potatoes, bread, cereals, pasta, rice and beans every day.

2 Water is essential for life. It lubricates and hydrates the body's organs and transports wastes. Drink at least six glasses of water per day, and more if you do hard physical exercise.

3 If you want to lose weight, you should eat a low-fat diet, but some fat is necessary. Fat provides energy, helps in the growth and repair of tissues and transports vitamins and minerals through the body.

4 If you're trying to lose weight and you get very hungry before mealtime, eat a low-calorie healthy snack like an apple or a low-fat yogurt. If you're too hungry at mealtime, you'll probably eat too much!

5 Eat as little as possible to lose weight, right? Wrong! You shouldn't feel hungry all the time. If you eat too little, your body thinks you're going to starve to death and it conserves fat. You have to eat to lose weight!

6 For the average person to keep fit, he/she probably needs to exercise for at least half an hour three times a week. Of course, this is the minimum, and your exercise program depends on your fitness goals, but it isn't necessary to over-exercise to keep fit.

7-8 Most people worry about being overweight. But being underweight can cause severe health problems, too. Very underweight people have a higher risk of death from heart diseases than average or overweight people. Brain functions can also be affected by being under weight. Finally, underweight people suffer from more bone fractures than average or overweight people.

3 Writing and listening

a Read the questions on Dr. Reed's website. Write answers to the questions.

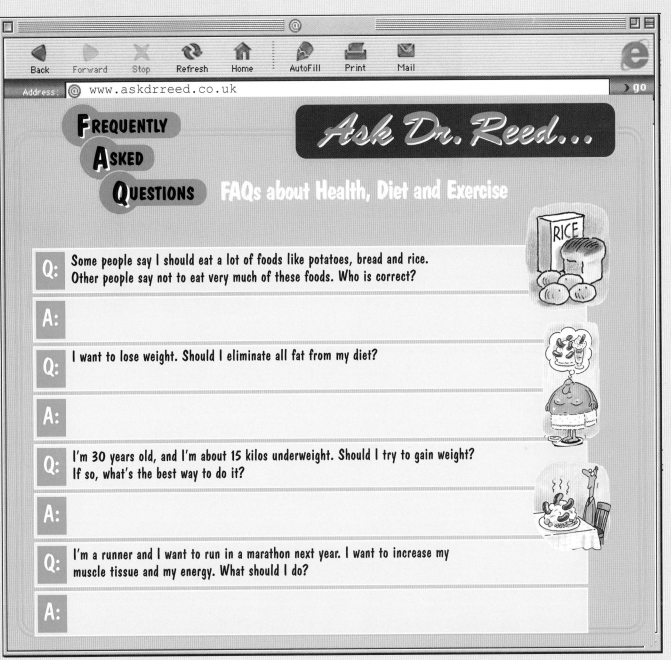

FREQUENTLY
ASKED
QUESTIONS

Ask Dr. Reed...

FAQs about Health, Diet and Exercise

Q: Some people say I should eat a lot of foods like potatoes, bread and rice. Other people say not to eat very much of these foods. Who is correct?

A:

Q: I want to lose weight. Should I eliminate all fat from my diet?

A:

Q: I'm 30 years old, and I'm about 15 kilos underweight. Should I try to gain weight? If so, what's the best way to do it?

A:

Q: I'm a runner and I want to run in a marathon next year. I want to increase my muscle tissue and my energy. What should I do?

A:

b Listen to Dr. Reed and compare his answers with yours.

4 Speaking

a Write one or two questions about health, diet and fitness.

I want to start running. How often and how far should I run?

b In groups, ask your questions.
Listen to your group's opinions on the answers.

Unit 4 City life

1 Immigrants

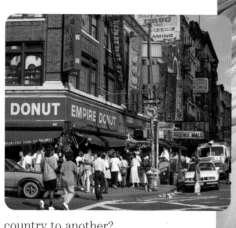

1 Speaking

Look at the photographs.

1 Why do you think people emigrate from one country to another?
2 What are the effects of immigration on a country like the U.S.?

2 Reading

a Read the article quickly and check your answers to exercise 1.

 The United States is a country formed by immigrants. Between 1850 and 1930 it took in about 35 million people. Of those people, 6 million came from Germany, about 5 million each from Italy and Ireland (1.5 million more than live in Ireland today), 3.3 million from Russia and 2.5 million from Scandinavia.

In 1890, 4 out of 5 people in New York City were either foreign born or the children of immigrants. Why did so many people come? Mainly to escape from poverty in their own countries, and in some cases as a result of persecution for religious or political beliefs.

In the last half of the 20th century, immigration slowed. In 1997, the United States received a total of 798,378 immigrants. Many of these came from Mexico (147,000), Southeast Asia (128,000) and the Caribbean (about 110,000).

The results of immigration can be seen in the number of foreign words in English and in the food and cosmopolitan culture of the United States. There are also many famous immigrants or children of immigrants including Charlie Chaplin (British), Albert Einstein (German), Alexander Graham Bell (Scottish), Madonna (Italian), Arnold Schwarzenegger (Austrian) and Monica Seles (Czech).

b Now read the article again and answer the questions.

1 What was surprising about the population in New York at the end of the 19th century?
2 What were the main reasons for immigration to the U.S.?
3 Where have immigrants mostly come from since the 1950s?
4 What are the main influences of immigration?

c Complete the information in the chart.

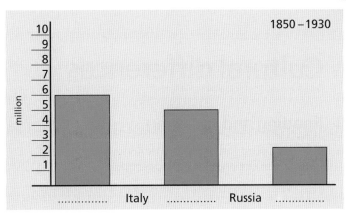

3 Word builder: origin of words

Many English words come from other languages. These are called "loan" words.

a Match the words with their language of origin.

1 rodeo ..f..   2 espresso .....   3 delicatessen .....   4 bagel .....   5 hooligan .....   6 cookie .....

a) Italian   b) Yiddish   c) Dutch   d) Gaelic (Irish)   e) German   f) Spanish

b Where do you think these words come from?

> sorbet   café   pizza   chocolate   denim

c Do you know any "loan" words in your language? Make a list with a partner.

4 Listening

a Listen and match the people with their country of origin.

1 Eva .....   2 Li .....   3 David .....   4 Rita .....   5 Laura .....

a) India   b) Cuba   c) China   d) Colombia   e) Poland

b Now listen again and write down the reasons why each person came to the U.S.

Eva   *She won a scholarship to study information technology.*

1 Li ....

2 David ....

3 Rita ....

4 Laura ....

5 Speaking

In groups, discuss these questions.

1 Has there been any immigration to your country? Where did the immigrants come from?

2 Why did these groups come to your country and what effects have they had?

3 Do you know any immigrants or children of immigrants? If yes, where are they from originally?

2 Cultural differences

1 Reading and speaking

culture shock /ˈkʌltʃər ʃɑk/: a feeling of anxiety, loneliness and confusion that people sometimes experience when they first arrive in another country or live with people from another culture.

a In groups, read the dictionary definition and discuss what kinds of things could cause culture shock.

The customs in another country are very different.

b In these cartoons, the people don't understand some of the customs in English-speaking countries! Match the cartoons with the customs.

1 People generally respect lines and will form lines when waiting for something. To push into a line will probably generate both anger and verbal complaints.

2 Direct eye contact in both social and business situations is important. No eye contact implies boredom or disinterest.

3 Many people become uncomfortable with periods of silence and will try to fill them with conversation.

4 You don't sit or stand very close to another person when having a conversation.

5 You must arrive on time for social and business appointments. Arriving late is normally unacceptable.

6 It is important to ask for permission from your host or hostess before smoking.

c In groups, discuss the cartoons. Which of the customs would be different or similar in your country?

2 Listening

a Listen to these people talking and match them with their cities.

1 Claudia López   a) New York
2 Tri Van Hong   b) Houston
3 Tatiana Tereschkova c) San Francisco

b Listen again and complete the information in the table.

Name	Country of origin	Present activity	Time doing this activity	Biggest cultural difference
Claudia López	Venezuela			
Tri Van Hong		Pharmacist		
Tatiana Tereschkova				People give lots of personal information

c In groups, compare your answers.

The biggest cultural difference for Tatiana is that ...

3 Grammar builder: review of present perfect vs. past simple

a Match the tenses with the rules.

1 Use this tense with a specific time or date in the past, or with *ago*.
2 Use this tense with *for* or *since* or with an unspecified time in the past.

a) present perfect
b) past simple

b Complete the paragraph using the correct form of the verb in parentheses.

My name is Claudia López and I'm from Venezuela. My husband and I (1) .... (*move*) to Houston, Texas, last January, so I (2) .... (*live*) in the U.S. for six months. I (3) .... (*get*) a job with a publicity company two months ago and I (4) .... (*work*) there since April. I need to speak good English for my job, so I (5) .... (*take*) English classes since I arrived in the U.S. There are a lot of nice people in my class and I (6) .... (*make*) some new friends. Last week we (7) .... (*have*) a class picnic and it (8) .... (*be*) a lot of fun.

4 Speaking

In groups, talk about your studies, work and hobbies.

A: *I study French.*
B: *How long have you studied it?*
A: *For about three years.*
B: *Have you ever been to France?*
A: *No, but I've been to Quebec.*
B: *Really? When did you go there?*
A: *Last summer.*

3 City versus country

1 Listening and reading

a Listen to Mike and Cathy talking to a newspaper reporter about life in the city compared to life in the country.

1 Which does Mike prefer?
2 Which does Cathy prefer?

Write their preferences under their names in the table.

b Listen again. Mark the categories P (positive) or N (negative).

	Environment	Crime	Cost	Transportation	Culture	Shopping	Facilities
Mike: (.........)							
Cathy: (.........)							

c Read the article and check your answers.

LIFESTYLE LIFESTYLE LIFESTYLE

This week in Lifestyle we have two very different views on city life compared to life in a small town. Mike Larson lives in a small town and he thinks the quality of life there is much better than in a big city. In Mike's opinion, a small town is peaceful, and it's a clean, safe environment, especially for children. People are very friendly and there aren't too many problems with crime. And of course, a small town is less expensive than a big city.

But Mike says there are some disadvantages to living in a small town. There aren't enough activities for young people and there aren't many stores and shops. Public facilities aren't very good either. The school in his town isn't big enough to provide everything the children need, and there isn't a hospital. But Mike says, "I like living in a small town - and I'm too old to move anyway!"

Cathy Ramos, on the other hand, says the city is the place for her. The city has the best facilities: schools and colleges, hospitals, etc. It also has excellent shopping malls and department stores. Culturally, the city is wonderful because there are many good museums, art galleries, theaters, clubs and restaurants. There's also plenty of transportation: buses, subways and taxis, and the airport is near the city.

Cathy says of course, there are problems in a big city. There's too much traffic and it's definitely more expensive than a small town. There's more crime, and it isn't as clean as the country. But she says she's a city girl and big cities are wonderful!

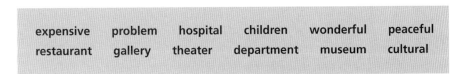

2 **Pronunciation:** word stress

a Listen to these words from exercise 1. Then write them in the correct column according to their stress pattern.

expensive	problem	hospital	children	wonderful	peaceful
restaurant	gallery	theater	department	museum	cultural

1) oOo	2) Oo	3) Ooo
expensive	problem	hospital

b Listen again and check.

3 **Grammar builder:** *too* and *enough; too much / too many*

a Look at these examples and answer the questions.

*The market is nice **enough**.*   *I'm **too** old to move.*
*There aren't **enough** parks.*   *There's **too much** traffic.*
*The school isn't big **enough**.*   *There aren't **too many** problems with crime.*

1 Are *too* and *enough* used before or after an adjective?
2 Is *enough* used before or after a noun?
3 What is the rule for using *too much* and *too many*?
4 How would you say the sentences in your language?

b Complete the paragraph using *too, too much, too many* or *enough*.

The new shopping mall is really great. There are lots of different stores and the main department store has three floors. But there are always (1) .... people and the parking lot isn't big (2) .... On the weekend it's (3) .... crowded to move. You have to line up for everything. Also, this mall isn't cheap and most people don't have (4) .... money to buy much there. There's a food court, but there's usually (5) .... noise to have a decent conversation. Perhaps it isn't such a great place after all!

4 **Writing and speaking**

a Write your opinions about life in a big city compared to life in the country or a small town. Use *enough, too (much / many)* and comparatives.

Cities are too noisy. The country is more relaxing than the city.

b In groups, take a class survey. How many people prefer cities? How many prefer small towns or the country?

4 Lifeline to urban planning

1 Reading and speaking

a In groups, look at the information in the charts and maps below and discuss these questions.

1 How has world population distribution changed in recent history?

2 What is expected to happen by 2025?

3 In your opinion, why have the world's megacities grown so fast?

4 What kinds of problems will these cities have to deal with?

b Now read the rest of the article and check your ideas.

The World's Biggest Cities

In the past, the vast majority of the world's population lived in rural areas or small communities. Most people worked in agriculture or in areas related to agriculture. But in the 19th century, this began to change in areas like Europe and the United States, where the Industrial Revolution brought more and more people to the cities to work in industry and services. As the Industrial Revolution spread to other countries, the move from country to city became a world-wide tendency. People believed, and still believe, that there are more opportunities in big cities than in rural

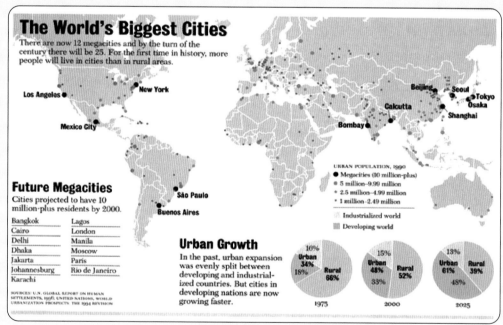

The World's Biggest Cities
There are now 12 megacities and by the turn of the century there will be 25. For the first time in history, more people will live in cities than in rural areas.

Future Megacities
Cities projected to have 10 million-plus residents by 2000.

Bangkok	Lagos
Cairo	London
Delhi	Manila
Dhaka	Moscow
Jakarta	Paris
Johannesburg	Rio de Janeiro
Karachi	

SOURCES: U.N. GLOBAL REPORT ON HUMAN SETTLEMENTS, 1996; UNITED NATIONS, WORLD URBANIZATION PROSPECTS: THE 1994 REVISION

URBAN POPULATION, 1990
● Megacities (10 million-plus)
● 5 million–9.99 million
● 2.5 million–4.99 million
· 1 million–2.49 million

Industrialized world
Developing world

Urban Growth
In the past, urban expansion was evenly split between developing and industrialized countries. But cities in developing nations are now growing faster.

1975 — Urban 34%, Rural 66%, 16% / 18%
2000 — Urban 48%, Rural 52%, 15% / 33%
2025 — Urban 61%, Rural 39%, 13% / 48%

areas. By 2025, sixty-one percent of the world's population will live in urban areas. There are, of course, problems associated with rapid urbanization. Many countries don't have enough money to provide the infrastructure necessary to support an enormous population in their cities. There are not enough public facilities like hospitals, schools and roads. Traffic is a huge problem, and vehicles cause pollution. Sometimes there isn't enough water for the needs of the population. Often the police are not prepared to combat the large amount of crime in a big city. If urbanization continues as predicted, there will be more and more problems in the world's megacities.

2 Reading and speaking

a **Read these facts quickly and match the topics with the texts.**

1   Housing   ◯   4   Trash dumping   ◯

2   Traffic congestion ◯   5   Water pollution   ◯

3   Air pollution   ◯   6   Insufficient electricity ◯

A India's capital, New Delhi, often turns off the electricity for more than six hours a day to stop the electric system from collapsing.

D In 1995, 20% of the planet's people did not have access to clean drinking water.

B Air pollution in Shanghai, China, is so heavy that it is comparable to smoking 20 to 30 cigarettes a day.

E A quarter of the population in the city of Dhaka, Bangladesh, live in slums.

C 300,000 new vehicles are added to the streets of Bangkok every year. The average Thai driver spends 44 full days a year sitting in traffic jams.

F Tokyo buries its garbage in artificial islands in Tokyo Bay and surrounding areas. But it will soon run out of room for the 5.5 million tons of household garbage it generates every year.

b **Read the facts again. Mark the statements T (true) or F (false).**

1   In New Delhi they sometimes cut off the electricity all day.   T ◯   F ◯

2   Air quality in Shanghai is very poor.   T ◯   F ◯

3   Every Thai driver spends more than a month each year in traffic jams. T ◯   F ◯

4   A quarter of the world's population cannot get clean water.   T ◯   F ◯

5   Access to decent housing is a major problem in Dhaka.   T ◯   F ◯

6   Tokyo has plenty of space for garbage.   T ◯   F ◯

3 Writing and speaking

a **In groups, imagine you are city planners.**
First, decide what the main problems of your city or town are and write them down.

There isn't enough water for the population.

Then write suggestions for solving the problems.

We should have rainwater collection systems for companies and public buildings.
These could provide more water for the city.

b **Compare your suggestions with other groups.**

Checkpoint 2

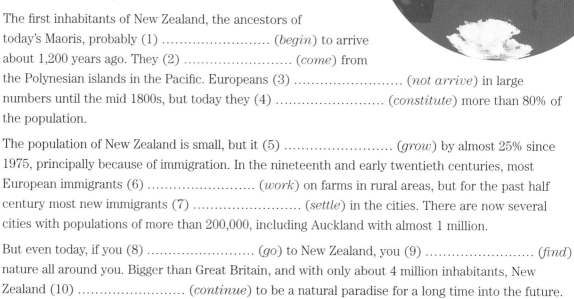

1 Check your progress

a Complete the text using the correct form of the verb in parentheses.

The first inhabitants of New Zealand, the ancestors of today's Maoris, probably (1) .... (*begin*) to arrive about 1,200 years ago. They (2) .... (*come*) from the Polynesian islands in the Pacific. Europeans (3) .... (*not arrive*) in large numbers until the mid 1800s, but today they (4) .... (*constitute*) more than 80% of the population.

The population of New Zealand is small, but it (5) .... (*grow*) by almost 25% since 1975, principally because of immigration. In the nineteenth and early twentieth centuries, most European immigrants (6) .... (*work*) on farms in rural areas, but for the past half century most new immigrants (7) .... (*settle*) in the cities. There are now several cities with populations of more than 200,000, including Auckland with almost 1 million.

But even today, if you (8) .... (*go*) to New Zealand, you (9) .... (*find*) nature all around you. Bigger than Great Britain, and with only about 4 million inhabitants, New Zealand (10) .... (*continue*) to be a natural paradise for a long time into the future.

b Complete the conversation using words or phrases from the box.
You can use the same word or phrase twice.
There are extra words and phrases.

came	come	did	enough	going to	has
have	too	too many	too much	will	won't

John: When did you (11) .... to New Zealand from Turkey, Kemal?

Kemal: Twelve years ago. Istanbul was (12) .... big to live in comfortably, and there was (13) .... noise and smog. And the biggest problem was that there weren't (14) .... jobs for all the young people. I (15) .... to New Zealand looking for new opportunities.

John: And (16) .... you find them?

Kemal: Yes. I have a good job and a nice house – it's small, but it's big (17) .... for my family.

John: (18) .... you been back to Turkey?

Kemal: Yes, twice. It's great to see the family and friends again.

John: Do you think Auckland (19) .... be like Istanbul one day, big, noisy and smoggy?

Kemal: No, I don't think so. But with all the immigrants like me, it's (20) .... grow a lot.

Score out of 20

○ 18–20 Excellent! ○ 15–17 Very good! ○ 12–14 OK, but review. ○ 9–11 You have some problems. Review units 3 and 4. ○ 0–8 Talk to your teacher.

40

2 Games to play

Form two teams. The teacher shows a member of Team A a situation described on a piece of paper.
Student A, mime the situation.
Team A, guess what is going to happen.
If you guess correctly, you get a point.
Repeat with Team B.

Examples of situations:

You're ...

... on a plane that is going to crash.

... going to take an important examination.

... up a tall tree and you're going to fall.

... going to have a baby in about a month.

... in prison and you're going to be free in an hour.

... going to change a baby's diaper.

... going to go out into the pouring rain.

3 My world

a **Think of your favorite city (apart from where you live now).**

1 How many times have you visited the city?

2 Why have you visited it?

3 When was the last time you went there?

4 Why do you like it?

5 Would you like to live there?

b **In pairs or groups, talk about your favorite cities.**

4 Personal word bank

a **Write as many nouns and adjectives as you can in the appropriate column in each table.**

The city		The country	
Nouns	**Adjectives**	**Nouns**	**Adjectives**
skyscraper	noisy	field	interesting

b **In pairs or groups, compare your words and, if necessary, explain why you chose them.**

A: Do you really think the country is interesting? I think it's boring.

B: No. There are lots of things to see and do. Traveling on a city bus every day is boring.

Unit 5 Fortunes

1 The lottery of life

1 Speaking

In groups, discuss the following questions.

1 Are there lotteries in your country? What are the biggest lotteries?

2 Are you a lucky person? Have you ever won a prize?

3 Have you ever won money in a lottery, or do you know anyone who has?

4 What are the good things and bad things about lotteries?

2 Reading, writing and speaking

a Read the stories about real lottery winners and answer the questions.

1 Where did James Jones use to work?
2 What did he buy?
3 What did Martin Davis do before he retired?
4 What is the biggest jackpot ever?
5 How much did Frank Carter win?

b Imagine you have won a big lottery prize. Write a list of presents you're going to give.

I'm going to buy my boyfriend a BMW, and give him a new watch – he's always late.

I'm going to give my parents a vacation in Europe and I want to buy them ...

c In pairs, compare and discuss your lists.

LOTTERY WINNERS

There are lots of different lotteries in the U.S., and lots of winners' stories. Here are just a few.

★

James Jones from Tennessee, used to work for McDonald's. Then he won $40 million in the lottery. He bought a new car and retired. All he wanted to do was relax and give money to his family.

★

Before 2000, the biggest prize ever was $104 million. Martin Davis was a 67-year-old retired truck driver. He worked part-time cutting grass at a local country club. After

taxes, he and his wife, Martha, won $67,940,000!

★

In 2000, The Big Game, a multi-state lottery, had a jackpot of $363 million – two people shared that, winning $181,500,000 each.

★

Finally, a very lucky man was Frank Carter from California. In fact, he was lucky three times! He first won $10,000 in April, 1998. Then he won $1 million in May, 1998 and finally he won $40,000 in January, 1999. Most people only dream of winning the lottery once!

★

3 **Word builder:** collocations

a **Match the following verbs with their definitions.**

1 earn   **a)** be unable to find, or no longer have something; fail in a competition

2 gain   **b)** obtain or deserve something through work or effort

3 win   **c)** obtain something through good luck, or in a competition

4 lose   **d)** use something inefficiently, or fail to take advantage of something

5 miss   **e)** increase, or obtain more of something

6 waste   **f)** fail to catch transportation, hit a target, or take an opportunity; feel sorry about the absence of someone or something

b **Write the correct form of the verbs from part a in the following sentences.**

1 We caught the bus to the station, but it arrived there late, and we almost .... the train.

2 While I was working, I lost three kilos. Now that I'm on vacation, I'm beginning to .... weight.

3 He practiced hard every day, but he didn't .... the competition. He came in third.

4 Don't .... your money on things you'll never use.

5 Many people work hard, but only .... enough money for their basic needs.

6 We often don't appreciate health, love or money, but we always .... them when we don't have them.

7 I .... my wallet, so I couldn't pay for my dinner.

4 **Writing and speaking**

a **Use these words from exercise 3 to write six sentences about things you have done or will do in the future.**

earn	gain	win	lose	miss	waste

I want to win enough money to buy a powerboat.

I won a 100 meter race at school in 1998.

b **In groups, talk about your experiences and ideas. Ask your classmates for more information.**

What countries do you want to visit?

2 Born to shop?

1 Speaking and reading

a The following article is about compulsive shoppers, or "shopaholics." In your opinion, what is a shopaholic?

b Read the article and match the topics with the paragraphs.

1 A historical reference to compulsive buying. paragraph ......

2 Recommendations for treatment of compulsive shopping. paragraph ......

3 An example of a compulsive shopper. paragraph ......

4 A definition of compulsive shopping. paragraph ......

SHOPPING - Necessity, Hobby ... or Illness?

1 For most people, the name Imelda Marcos probably brings one image to mind – shoes. The wife of Philippino ex-president Ferdinand Marcos was famous for her shoe collection. She owned 3,000 pairs of shoes, including a pair of plastic disco sandals with battery-operated flashing lights in the 8 cm. heels! An advertisement in the window of a New York shoe shop said, "There is a little Imelda in all of us."

2 But is there? Does anyone *need* 3,000 pairs of shoes? Of course not, but many people buy things not because they need them, but impulsively, simply for the fun of buying. Like alcoholism or drug abuse, shopping can become an addiction, and compulsive shoppers can't stop themselves from buying things. It isn't just silly behavior; it is a psychological illness.

3 Compulsive shopping isn't a new phenomenon. A German psychiatrist identified it nearly 100 years ago, and called it oniomania (buying mania). Today, we often refer to people who keep shopping as "shopaholics." Estimates indicate that 2–8% of Americans are compulsive shoppers.

4 Many psychiatrists are now working to help compulsive shoppers recognize their problem and understand what makes them spend money. Some psychiatrists recommend anti-depressant drugs like Prozac, but most prefer non-drug therapies. They first tell people to analyze why they shop – a feeling of power, low self-esteem, etc. Then they advise them to keep a daily record of all the money they spend. Finally, they encourage people to look for alternate forms of entertainment – reading, exercising, etc.

2 Grammar builder: verb complementation

a Underline these verbs in the article in exercise 1. Then write them in the appropriate tables below.

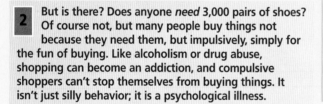

help	advise	tell	stop	encourage	make

1) Parents   *let*   children do ...

3) Money problems   *prevent*   people (from) doing ...

2) We should *allow*   people to do ...

b Complete the sentences using verbs from the tables on page 44.

1 Advertising sometimes .... us buy things we don't need.
2 Parents shouldn't .... their children shop without supervision.
3 If you know someone who spends too much money, ... him/her to save.
4 The government shouldn't .... lotteries to advertise.
5 We should .... people from wasting money on the lottery.

c In groups, discuss whether you agree or disagree with the above statements.

3 Pronunciation: word stress

a Listen to these sentences. Underline the stressed syllable in the words in bold.

1 My parents **advised** me to go to college.
2 We should **prevent** children from watching violent movies.
3 This restaurant doesn't **allow** people to smoke.
4 Parents should **encourage** children to read.

b Listen again and practice the sentences.

4 Reading and speaking

a Answer the questions in this mini-quiz to find out how careful you are with money.

1	*When I have extra money, I a) almost always spend it.* *b) rarely*
2	*I a) usually spend my free time in stores and malls.* *b) rarely*
3	*I a) always check the price of things I buy.* *b) never*
4	*I a) rarely buy things I don't need.* *b) often*
5	*I am a) conscious of the cost of services like water.* *b) not conscious*
6	*I a) rarely eat in restaurants.* *b) often*

b Look at your answers to the quiz. In pairs, discuss these questions.

1 Do you think you are careful with money and manage it well?
2 Why? / Why not?

3 Money, money, money

1 Word builder: money

Match the words with their definitions.

1 money   a) round, flat pieces of metal used to buy things

2 salary   b) a place that makes coins and/or bills

3 coins   c) to give money in exchange for work or products

4 bills   d) money that a person receives for work

5 mint   e) coins or bills that have value for buying things

6 to be worth   f) paper money

7 to pay   g) to have value

2 Speaking and listening

a **Read the statements. Do you think they are correct?**

1 The word "money" comes from the name of a Roman goddess.

2 The word "salary" comes from the verb "sell."

3 The expression "He isn't worth his salt" means "He works very well."

b **Listen and check your ideas.**

c **Listen again and mark the sentences T (true) or F (false).**

1 The Roman mint was next to a temple to the god Jupiter.   T ◯   F ◯

2 People were using coins more than 300 years before Christ.   T ◯   F ◯

3 The Roman mint made coins and bills.   T ◯   F ◯

4 The Romans used to pay people with salt.   T ◯   F ◯

5 One student in the class says he would like to be paid in salt.   T ◯   F ◯

6 The students are going to read an article about money.   T ◯   F ◯

3 Reading

a **In pairs, number the sentences in the correct historical order.**

1...... Asians started using coins.

2......The Romans built a mint for making coins.

3...1...The Chinese used knives and rice as money.

4......Native Americans used beads and furs as money.

5......The Chinese invented paper money.

6......Europeans started using paper money.

b Now read the article and check your answers.

The History of Money

There haven't always been coins and bills – money as we know it. In ancient times, people used objects to trade for things they needed. For example, 3,000 years before Christ, the Chinese were using knives and rice as money because these things were very valuable.

Then, in about 600 B.C., people started making coins out of gold, silver and other metals. That was in the area of Asia we now call Turkey and also in China. In about 390 B.C., the Romans built a mint for making coins.

For hundreds of years, people only used coins, but coins were heavy, and it was dangerous to travel with a lot of gold and silver, so finally paper money was invented. The first paper money was used in China, around 810 A.D. Europeans started using it in about 1000 A.D. Of course, not everyone had paper money or coins at that time.

In 1600 A.D., Native Americans were still using beads and furs as money. In 1624, they traded the island of Manhattan to the Dutch for goods worth $24 at today's value!

4 Grammar builder: reasons and purposes

a Look at these sentences. They all answer the question *Why*.
Which pair of sentences gives a reason for doing something and which pair gives a purpose?

1 a) The Romans built a mint **so that** they could make coins.

   b) The Romans built a mint **to** make coins.

2 a) The Chinese invented paper money **because** they didn't want to carry gold and silver.

   b) The Chinese didn't want to carry gold and silver, **so** they invented paper money.

b Complete the second sentence so that it means the same as the first sentence.

1 There is high inflation, so prices increase constantly.
   Prices increase constantly ....

2 I couldn't buy a car because I didn't have enough money.
   I didn't have enough money, ...

3 I want to get a Master's degree so that I can get a good job.
   I want to get a Master's degree ....

4 We opened a savings account to save money for an apartment.
   We opened a savings account ....

5 Writing and speaking

a Write several sentences about things you have done or plan to do to help your financial situation.

Last month I cancelled my credit cards. I'm going to change my job.

b In groups, talk about your sentences.

   A: I cancelled all my credit cards.
   B: Why?
   A: So that I wouldn't spend so much money.

4 Lifeline to economics

1 Speaking and listening

a In pairs, agree on a definition of "inflation." Compare your definition with another pair.

b Listen to part of a college economics class, and check your definition.

c Listen again and complete this student's notes.

> Inflation   = general rate of (1) ....
>
> 1–5%   = typical inflation now in (2) ....
>
> 1,300 billion% = highest rate of inflation this century, in (3) .... in (4) 19 .....

2 Speaking

In groups, discuss the annual variation in the cost of products and services in your country.
Use the questions in the box to help you.

Consider these items. How much do they cost now, and how much did they cost at this time last year?

Do you think inflation is high, moderate or low?

Do you know the official rate of inflation in your country?

3 Speaking and reading

a In groups, discuss these questions.

1 How much would you pay for these products? Write a price for each one and compare your answers with a partner.

     a) a hamburger ......   **b)** a watch ......   **c)** sneakers ......   **d)** jeans ......   **e)** a soft drink ......

2 How important is a brand name to you?
Are certain brands better than others, or just more expensive?

3 Can companies help give their products prestige by selling them at high prices?
For what kinds of products might this strategy work?

b **Are these statements T (true) or F (false)? Read the report to check your answers.**

1 Prices can vary almost 75% for the same product.   T ◯ F ◯

2 People usually buy things like detergent on the basis of brand name.   T ◯ F ◯

3 Price can be influenced by consumer perception of a brand.   T ◯ F ◯

4 Companies like Rolex and Gucci market their products primarily on the basis of price.   T ◯ F ◯

5 Some people buy certain products because they're more expensive.   T ◯ F ◯

Prices can vary a lot, even for the same product. For example, you pay 27 cents for a cola in the supermarket, 44 cents for the same cola from a dispensing machine and as much as 99 cents for a cola in a restaurant. Why are the prices so different? In the case of the cola, prices are affected by volume.

A supermarket, for example, buys large amounts of a product and so can sell it more cheaply than restaurants.

But pricing is also affected by what we're prepared to pay. Consumers won't pay a lot for certain things, like detergent or paper towels. They often choose these products only on the basis of price. Would you pay $10.00 for a hamburger? Probably not. But would you pay $60.00 for a pair of sneakers? It depends. If the shoes are a well-known brand, you would probably pay that much. If they were sneakers in the supermarket, you probably wouldn't. In this case, price is influenced by the consumer's perception of the brand. People will pay more for certain exclusive brands like Rolex watches, Ferrari cars, Gucci bags and Calvin Klein jeans because they perceive more value in them. Finally, people buy certain brands, even if (or because) they are more expensive because they give a feeling of prestige and of being different. For example, buying a Rolls Royce makes people feel special and part of an elite group.

c **In pairs, answer these questions.**

1 Why do prices for the same product vary?
2 Do people usually buy all products on the basis of price?
3 What is one reason exclusive brands cost more money?
4 What are two reasons why people buy very exclusive brands of products?

4 Writing and speaking

a **Complete the paragraph with your own ideas.**

When I shop, I usually buy … When I want to buy something, the most important factor is …

If a product is … I won't buy it. I usually shop at … so that …

I never shop at … because …

For me, shopping is …

b **Exchange paragraphs with a partner. Talk about your ideas.**

A: *You said you usually buy CDs or videos. Do you often buy clothes?*
B: *No, almost never. I hate trying on clothes.*

49

Unit 6 Entertainment

Entertainment at home

1 Speaking and listening

a In groups, think of as many types of home entertainment as you can (e.g. watching TV). What's the group's favorite type of home entertainment?

b Listen to three people talking about how they relax at home. Which three types of home entertainment are they talking about?

c Listen again and answer these questions.

1 Who does Jill like to "talk to" on her computer?
2 Where does Joe have his stereo system?
3 How many CDs does Joe buy every weekend?
4 What is Sue's favorite type of program?

2 Speaking and writing

a Talk to your classmates to find out what they do for entertainment. Write names next to the activities in the table.

A: *Do you play an instrument?*
B: *Yes, I do.*
A: *What do you play?*
B: *The guitar.*
A: *Oh, that's interesting. I know ...*

Find someone who ...	Name
plays a musical instrument	. . . .
tells a lot of jokes	. . . .
watches cable or satellite TV a lot	. . . .
uses the Internet for entertainment	. . . .
has been to a concert recently	. . . .
has read a good book recently	. . . .

b Choose one of the people you spoke to and write a short paragraph about his/her entertainment preferences.

I talked to Isabel. She doesn't play a musical instrument but she likes listening to music ...

3 Speaking and reading

a In pairs, discuss these questions.

1 Do you use the Internet?   2 Do many people you know use it?

3 What do you / your friends usually use it for?

b With your partner, read the web page and match the answers with the frequently asked questions (FAQs). Then check your ideas with another pair.

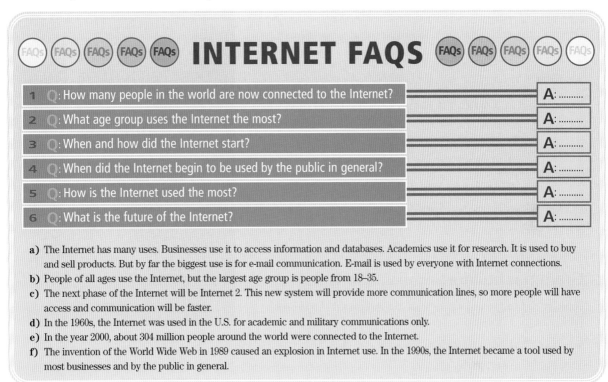

INTERNET FAQS

1 Q: How many people in the world are now connected to the Internet?   A: ....

2 Q: What age group uses the Internet the most?   A: ....

3 Q: When and how did the Internet start?   A: ....

4 Q: When did the Internet begin to be used by the public in general?   A: ....

5 Q: How is the Internet used the most?   A: ....

6 Q: What is the future of the Internet?   A: ....

a) The Internet has many uses. Businesses use it to access information and databases. Academics use it for research. It is used to buy and sell products. But by far the biggest use is for e-mail communication. E-mail is used by everyone with Internet connections.

b) People of all ages use the Internet, but the largest age group is people from 18–35.

c) The next phase of the Internet will be Internet 2. This new system will provide more communication lines, so more people will have access and communication will be faster.

d) In the 1960s, the Internet was used in the U.S. for academic and military communications only.

e) In the year 2000, about 304 million people around the world were connected to the Internet.

f) The invention of the World Wide Web in 1989 caused an explosion in Internet use. In the 1990s, the Internet became a tool used by most businesses and by the public in general.

4 Speaking

a In groups, find answers to the following questions.

1 Who in your group uses the Internet?

2 What do they use it for?

3 If people don't use the Internet, what would they use it for?

b Compare your group's results with the other groups.

Uses	Name	✓ / ✗	Name	✓ / ✗	Name	✓ / ✗	Name	✓ / ✗
e-mail								
chat rooms								
downloading music								
research								
buying things								
other ...								

2 Going out

1 Listening and speaking

a Can you name some famous places in New York?

b Listen to the conversation and answer these questions.

1 Where does the conversation take place?
2 What is the visitor asking about?

c Listen again and match the names with the types of place.

1 Hyatt ..c..
2 Metropolitan ......   **a)** museum
3 Guggenheim ......   **b)** restaurant-bar with live music
4 Rockefeller Plaza ...... **c)** hotel
5 Applause ......   **d)** ice-skating rink
6 O' Looney's ......

2 Grammar builder: indefinite pronouns

a Look at the following sentences. Underline all the words with ...*body*, ...*thing* or ...*where*.

1 Somebody in our group goes to the movies every week – Monica. Nobody goes to the theater.
2 I know somebody in television, but I don't know anybody in the movies. Do you know anybody?
3 I know somewhere good to eat, but I don't know anywhere to listen to live music.
4 James Bond saw there was something on the floor beside the body – a small box. He opened it – there wasn't anything inside.

b Answer the questions.

1 Which words do you use with questions and negatives?
2 Can you use *nobody* or *nothing* in a question or negative?

c Complete the table with the words in the box.

somebody   nobody   anybody   something   nothing   anything
somewhere   nowhere   anywhere

People		Places		Things	
Affirmative	**Negative**	**Affirmative**	**Negative**	**Affirmative**	**Negative**

d Complete this conversation from a TV comedy program.

John: Ah, there's (1) .... on my desk. I wonder what it is.
Hmm, it's a box. But there's (2) .... in it.
It's completely empty. There should be a label
on it (3) ....

Sue: What's in that box, John? (4) .... interesting?

John: No, it's empty. (5) .... left it here on my desk.
Who could it be? Did you see (6) .... come
into my office while I was out, Sue?

Sue: Of course I didn't see (7) ...., John.
(8) .... ever goes into your office when
you're out ... that's a nice tie you're wearing.

John: What? Oh, yes, I bought it this morning ... It ... was ...

Sue: ... in that box?

John: Yes.

e Listen and check your answers.

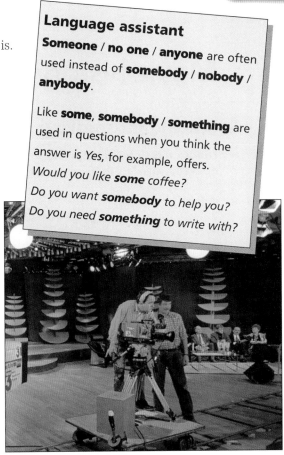

Language assistant

Someone / **no one** / **anyone** are often used instead of **somebody** / **nobody** / **anybody**.

Like **some**, **somebody** / **something** are used in questions when you think the answer is *Yes*, for example, offers.
Would you like **some** *coffee?*
Do you want **somebody** *to help you?*
Do you need **something** *to write with?*

3 Pronunciation: sounds – "o" as /ʌ/ or /oʊ/

a Listen to these sounds.

1 /ʌ/ son, mother

2 /oʊ/ home, hotel

b Listen and number the words 1 or 2 according
to the sound.

somebody ..1.. nobody ..2.. someone ......

nothing ...... somewhere ...... nowhere ......

brother ...... cousin ...... go ...... don't ......

does ...... no ...... money ...... know ......

c Listen and repeat these sentences. Then practice them in pairs.

1 My brother loves someone in London.

2 Nobody goes home alone.

3 My mother knows most of her cousins.

4 Joan goes nowhere and does nothing.

4 Speaking

In groups, discuss places to go and things to do in your city.

A: I want to do something exciting / go somewhere nice / meet someone interesting this weekend.
B: Why don't you go to Matrix? It's a great place and it has good music.

3 Movie history

1 Reading and speaking

a Look at these photographs. In pairs, try to guess the answers to these questions.

1 Who were these people?
2 When were they in the movies?
3 Where were they from?
4 Are they still alive?

b Now read about Mary Pickford and Rudolph Valentino and check your answers.

Gladys Marie Smith was born in Toronto, Canada, in 1892. At 16, she starred in her first Hollywood movie under her professional name, Mary Pickford. The following year she appeared in 51 movies – silent ones, with no script to learn. She soon became "America's Sweetheart," the girl everyone loved. She was also a founder of the Academy of Motion Picture Arts and Sciences. That is the association which awards the Oscars. In 1976 she was awarded an Oscar for Lifetime Achievement. She died on May 29, 1979, in Santa Monica, California, at the age of 87.

Rodolfo Alfonzo Raffaele Pierre Philibert Guglielmi di Valentina d'Antonguolla was born in Italy in 1895. In 1913 he left Italy to go to the U.S. and became Rudolph Valentino. He worked as a dancer in New York before going to Hollywood. *The Four Horsemen of the Apocalypse* (1921) was the movie that made him famous. He was a sensation because of his good looks, his intense expressions, his exaggerated movements and his tango dancing. *The Sheik* is the Valentino movie most people remember. It firmly established his position as the male movie idol of the time, the first great Latin Lover of the movies. Sadly, he died very young at the age of 31.

c Read the article again and say who each statement is about.

1 started acting in 1908 ....
2 founded the Oscar association ....
3 was born in Europe ....
4 was a great dancer ....
5 went to the U.S. at age 18 ....
6 won an Oscar at age 84 ....
7 was very good-looking ....
8 didn't live very long ....

d In groups, discuss these questions.

1 Can you think of other stars who made "movie history"?
2 Is there a movie industry in your country? Who are the past and present stars?
3 Have any actors from your country become stars in the U.S. or Europe? Who are they?

2 Speaking

In groups, think of a name for each category.

The first group to finish wins!

TRIVIA QUIZ

Name ...
1 a movie which won an Oscar for Best Picture
2 an actress who won an Oscar for Best Actress
3 a rock group which played in your country
4 a painting which sold for over $1 million
5 a TV personality who got married recently
6 a rock song which was Number 1 in the U.S.
7 a Russian dancer who was very famous
8 an actor who died very young

3 Grammar builder: relative clauses

a Look at these sentences and answer the questions.

There are two people in my class **that play the guitar**.

Mary Pickford was the silent movie star **who helped found the Academy**.

The Academy is the association **which awards the Oscars**.

The Four Horsemen of the Apocalypse *(1921) was the movie* **that made Valentino famous**.

1 Which relative clauses (in bold print) refer to people, and which refer to things?

2 Which word (*who, that,* or *which*) refers only to people?

3 Which word refers only to things?

4 Which word can refer to both people and things?

5 Are *who / which / that* followed by a verb or a noun?

b Complete these sentences with *who* or *which* (or *that*).

1 I like singers .... have style as well as a good voice.

2 A TV program .... seems to go on forever is *Cheers*.

3 A good comedy is something .... most people enjoy.

4 *Titanic* is the movie .... made the most money in the twentieth century.

5 People .... we don't see on the screen (e.g. writers) can be more important than the actors.

6 We need more actors .... are good at comedy as well as drama, like Mel Gibson.

4 Writing and speaking

a Complete the sentences for you.

1 I like music / movies that ...

2 I prefer actors who ...

3 I don't like actors that ...

4 I don't like TV programs which ...

b Now, in groups, talk about your opinions.

4 Lifeline to movie and TV production

1 Speaking and writing

a In pairs, write lists for these categories. Classify them as D (domestic productions made in your country), A (American productions) or O (other foreign productions).

1 The most popular programs on TV at the moment.

2 The movies showing at the moment.

b Compare your list with another pair, and discuss the information. What are your conclusions?

c Write your conclusions.

Most TV programs in our country are ... There are some ...
Most people seem to prefer ... The movies showing at the moment ...

2 Reading

a Read this article. Is the information similar to or different from your conclusions in exercise 1?

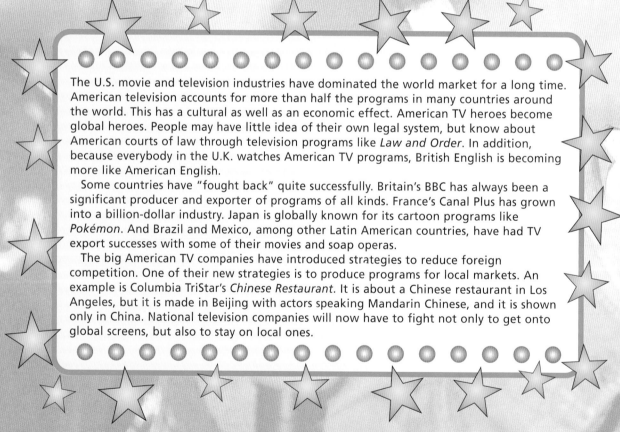

The U.S. movie and television industries have dominated the world market for a long time. American television accounts for more than half the programs in many countries around the world. This has a cultural as well as an economic effect. American TV heroes become global heroes. People may have little idea of their own legal system, but know about American courts of law through television programs like *Law and Order*. In addition, because everybody in the U.K. watches American TV programs, British English is becoming more like American English.

Some countries have "fought back" quite successfully. Britain's BBC has always been a significant producer and exporter of programs of all kinds. France's Canal Plus has grown into a billion-dollar industry. Japan is globally known for its cartoon programs like *Pokémon*. And Brazil and Mexico, among other Latin American countries, have had TV export successes with some of their movies and soap operas.

The big American TV companies have introduced strategies to reduce foreign competition. One of their new strategies is to produce programs for local markets. An example is Columbia TriStar's *Chinese Restaurant*. It is about a Chinese restaurant in Los Angeles, but it is made in Beijing with actors speaking Mandarin Chinese, and it is shown only in China. National television companies will now have to fight not only to get onto global screens, but also to stay on local ones.

b Read the article again. In pairs or groups, discuss and answer these questions.

1 What possible cultural effects of American TV does the article mention?

2 Which countries have been able to compete a little with American TV in foreign markets?

3 What is one of the strategies of American TV companies to reduce foreign competition?

4 Will it be easy or difficult for national TV companies to survive in their own countries?

56

3 Word builder: television vocabulary

a Write the words from the box in the appropriate column.

actor	actress	cable	cameraman	talk show	comedy	director	drama	lighting
microphone	news	producer	screen	script writer	set	documentary
soap (opera)	transmitter

People / Jobs	Types of programs	Equipment, etc.

b Match the beginnings with the ends of the definitions.

1 A talk show is a program in which
2 The director is the person who
3 The set is the place where
4 A documentary is a program that
5 A producer is the person who
6 A transmitter is an object that

a) is about real events.
b) the action in a movie or TV show happens.
c) sends the signals which reach your TV.
d) somebody interviews a famous person.
e) tells actors how to play their parts.
f) organizes everything related to a movie or TV show.

c Look back at the programs you listed in exercise 1. What kinds of programs are they?

4 Speaking

a In pairs, consider the following aspects of TV fiction (soaps, comedy and drama) in your country.
Check (✓) each aspect as good, average or bad in general.

	Good	Average	Bad
Ideas and scripts			
Direction and acting			
Locations, sets, costumes, etc.			
Camera work, lighting, effects, etc.			
Other:			

b Compare your evaluation with another pair. In general do you think TV
programs in your country are good, average or bad?

The scripts for comedies are usually very good, but sometimes the acting is only average.

Checkpoint 3

1 Check your progress

a Complete this conversation using one word in each space.

Marion: Hey, Chuck, do you know (1) .... who speaks Portuguese?

Chuck: No, I don't. I know (2) .... that speaks Spanish, Mary Ortega. But (3) ....
speaks Portuguese around here. Why?

Marion: Well, we need an interpreter (4) .... a young singer from Brazil is coming next
week. She's excellent, and we want her (5) .... sign a recording contract with us.

Chuck: But if she sings in Portuguese, how will you promote her?

Marion: No problem. She sounds great in Portuguese. She'll make everyone (6) .... to
learn the language.

Chuck: Well, it's a great language. Nothing is going to stop me from (7) .... it one of
these days.

Marion: Ha, one of these days! She sings in Spanish too, and there are millions of people
(8) .... buy Spanish language records here in the U.S.

Chuck: She speaks Spanish? Well, you should ask Mary Ortega (9) .... be your interpreter.

Marion: Yes! I'll call her right now (10) .... see if she's free next week.

b Match the first and second parts of these sentences to make a story.

11 The Brazilian singer comes from a city ...	a) ... to study with a famous singing teacher.
12 She wants to become more international ...	b) ... because her father made her study.
13 Her father is the person ...	c) ... anything interfere with their education.
14 He made her take piano lessons ...	d) ... that preferred soccer to piano lessons.
15 He was poor, but ...	e) ... study a minimum of two hours every night.
16 He wouldn't let ...	f) ... who encouraged her to take singing seriously.
17 He made them all ...	g) ... so that she would really understand music.
18 He sent Maria to Portugal ...	h) ... so she is coming to the U.S.
19 Maria was the kind of girl ...	i) ... which is very musical.
20 But she has really become successful ...	j) ... he did a lot for his children.

Score out of 20

◯ 18–20 Excellent!	◯ 15–17 Very good!	◯ 12–14 OK, but review.	◯ 9–11 You have some problems. Review units 5 and 6.	◯ 0–8 Talk to your teacher.

2 Games to play

Student A, write the name of a well-known person, e.g. Venus Williams, on a piece of paper. Other students, ask questions.

Is it somebody   who sings?
*   that acts in movies?*
*   who plays a sport?*
*   that lives in ...?*

When a student guesses correctly, Student A shows the paper with the name. The student who guessed then writes a new name on a piece of paper. Repeat the game.

3 My world

In groups, look at the pictures and discuss what you think about the following situations.

I don't think people should let animals ...

I agree. I think ...

I think parents should make their children ...

I don't agree. I think parents should encourage their children to ...

4 Personal word bank

a Match the first and second parts of the sentences to make logical sentences.

1 You can earn money ...	**a)** ... intelligently or stupidly.
2 You can win money ...	**b)** ... buying useless things.
3 You can save money ...	**c)** ... if you don't keep it in a safe place.
4 You can waste money ...	**d)** ... giving private English classes.
5 You can lose money ...	**e)** ... in talent contests.
6 You can spend money ...	**f)** ... using low energy light bulbs.

b Write sentences about other ways you can earn, win, save, waste or lose money. Compare your sentences with another student.

Unit 7 Living culture

1 Celebrations

1 Speaking

In groups, look at the photographs and answer the questions.

1 What do the photographs show?
2 Which photographs show more international events / people and which are more local?
3 What are some typical cultural activities in your country?

2 Listening and speaking

a Listen to two people talking about traditions in Mexico and check (✓) the topics they mention.

music	◯	clothes	◯
food	◯	festivals	◯
parties	◯	sports	◯

b Now listen again and complete the sentences.

1 Mole is a sauce made from ...., spices and .... and eaten with ....
2 The Day of the Dead is in .... Mexicans remember people who .... but there are funny things like .... skulls and special .... People leave offerings of .... and drink for the spirits.
3 When Mexican girls are ...., the families have a big .... to celebrate. There is often a .... service, too.

c What about your country? In groups, discuss the questions.

1 What's your favorite traditional food?
2 What festivals are there and when are these celebrated?
3 When do people have parties to celebrate something special?

3 Reading and speaking

a In pairs, mark the sentences T (true) or F (false).

1 Chinese New Year is celebrated on January 1.   T ○   F ○

2 Luck is an important concept in Chinese New Year celebrations.   T ○   F ○

3 San Fermín is a city in Spain.   T ○   F ○

4 The bulls run through the town every day for a week.   T ○   F ○

5 Samba schools specialize in music.   T ○   F ○

6 People used to throw water and eggs during Carnival.   T ○   F ○

b Now read the extracts and check your answers.

In China, the New Year is usually celebrated in February. In the days before the New Year, houses are cleaned and doors and window frames are painted red, which symbolizes good luck. On Chinese New Year's Eve, families have a big dinner with special foods for good luck. People wear red clothes, but no black or white because those colors symbolize death.

On New Year's Day married couples give money in red envelopes to children and unmarried adults. Two weeks later is the Festival of Lanterns, with singing, dancing and lantern shows. At midnight there is a big fireworks show.

Every year in Pamplona, Spain, the Fiesta of San Fermín is celebrated from July 7 to 14. Every day, bulls are released and they run through the streets of the town. Young men run in front of the bulls and try not to get injured. The distance is 800 meters and the run lasts only two minutes, but it's very dangerous. A bull weighs about 600 kilos and has two sharp horns. But the Running of the Bulls attracts thousands of people every year.

One of the biggest celebrations in Brazil is Carnival. Samba schools compete with each other for the best dancers, shows and costumes. Each school is made up of thousands of dancers in wonderful costumes and millions of dollars are spent every year on the show production. Originally, people celebrated Carnival by throwing water and eggs at each other, but since 1910 Carnival has been based on samba and dancing.

c In groups, talk about which of these celebrations you would like to go to and why.

4 Writing and speaking

a Write a short description of a festival in your country. Use the questions in the box to help you.

When is the festival?	Where is it held?	Why is it organized?	What happens?

Do you eat any special food or wear special clothes at the festival?

b Exchange descriptions with a partner. Read your partner's description. Talk about the festivals.

A: *What do you and your family usually do on Christmas?*
B: *We usually celebrate at my aunt's house. We have a big meal, and ...*

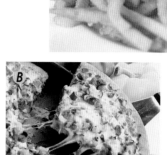

2 Culture on the table

1 Speaking

a In pairs, look at the different types of food and discuss these questions.

1 Which country do they come from?
2 What kind of fast food do you like?
3 Why do you think this type of food is so popular?

b Make a list of reasons and compare them with another pair of students.

2 Reading

a Read the article and complete the table.

Fast food pioneer

Which quick service restaurant chain has more than 26,000 restaurants in 119 countries, has a clown as its symbol and virtually invented the idea of fast food? You probably guessed it: McDonald's. The classic McDonald's meal is a hamburger with French fries and a drink. McDonald's hamburgers are made from 100% pure beef, which is cooked on a grill and served in a bun with onion, tomato ketchup, mustard and dill pickle.

Mac and Dick McDonald created the concept of quick service at their restaurant in San Bernardino, California. They also invented the idea of specialization – one person cooked the hamburgers, another made milkshakes and another put mayonnaise on the buns.
But the biggest innovation was to have the food prepared and waiting so customers could place an order and immediately collect it. The food was good and cheap and business exploded. People felt confident in taking their families because they could expect cleanliness and food of a certain quality.

Their business grew and by the mid 1950s, the original restaurant was making $350,000 a year. Then in 1954, Ray Kroc, an electric mixer salesman, visited the restaurant. In 1955, he opened a second McDonald's restaurant in Des Plaines, Illinois. He persuaded the brothers to open several other restaurants in other cities. Four years later he opened the 100th restaurant in Chicago. In 1961, Kroc bought all rights to the McDonald's concept from the McDonald brothers for $2.7 million.

McDonald's Fact File

1 Number of restaurants:

2 Inventors of McDonald's quick service system:

3 Where they opened their first restaurant:

4 Classic McDonald's meal:

5 Ingredients of McDonald's hamburger:

6 Ray Kroc's original job:

7 Amount paid by Ray Kroc for the business:

---

b Check your answers with a partner.

3 Grammar builder: present passive

a Look at these examples from the text and answer the questions.

Active
___

They **make** McDonald's hamburgers from 100% pure beef.

They **cook** the beef on a grill.

Passive
___

McDonald's hamburgers **are made** from 100% pure beef.

The beef **is cooked** on a grill.

---

1   How is the passive formed?
2   How is the passive voice different from the active voice?
3   Is there an equivalent to this structure in your language?
4   How does the present passive change in the singular and plural?

b Rewrite these sentences using the present passive. Look at the first example to help you.

*Americans **eat** thousands of hot dogs every year.*
    Thousands of hot dogs **are eaten** every year by Americans.

1   You make pizzas from tomato sauce, mozzarella cheese and dough.
2   The biggest companies spend millions of dollars on TV advertising.
3   Many people eat sushi because it's tasty and cheap.
4   Americans drink millions of liters of milk every year.
5   People sell Coca-Cola all over the world.

Language assistant

If the subject of a passive sentence is important, indicate the subject with *by*.
*Millions of hamburgers are **sold by McDonald's** every year.*

If the subject isn't important, you don't need to use *by*.
*Millions of hamburgers **are eaten** every year.*

4 Writing and speaking

a Write a description of a dish in your country. Use the expressions in the box to help you.

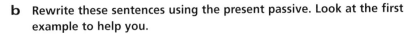

| This dish is made with ... | It comes from (region). | It is usually served with ... |
| It is eaten in (season) / on (festival). |

b In groups, read the descriptions. The group guesses the dishes.

3 Culture at home

1 Listening, writing and speaking

a Listen to Sandra talking to her friend, Luke. Answer these questions.

1 What is the topic of the conversation?
2 Why are they talking about this?

b Now listen again and complete the chart comparing the two countries.

	Same	Different
Language	....	....
Driving	....	....
Food	....	....
Weather	....	....
People	....	....

c In groups, compare your country with another country, using the categories above.

1 Write sentences comparing the two countries.
2 Tell your class about your comparisons.

The language is different. We speak Spanish here. In the U.S. they speak English.

2 Grammar builder: expressions followed by verb + -ing or to + verb

a Match the first and second part of the sentences.

1 I'm looking forward to
2 I'd like
3 I have trouble
4 I'm used to
5 I'll probably get used to
6 I mustn't forget

a) driving on the "wrong" side after a little practice.
b) to take an umbrella – it rains a lot.
c) visiting you next month.
d) understanding some people from Scotland and England.
e) to know more about different countries.
f) driving on the right.

b Classify the following expressions as:

1 normally followed by verb + -ing. 2 normally followed by to + verb.

be used to ......   forget ......   stop ......   decide ......

get used to ......   enjoy ......   have trouble ......   want ......

finish ......   look forward to ...... would like ......

3 **Pronunciation:** weak forms – verb + *to*

a Listen and repeat these sentences. How does *to* sound in them?

1 I'm looking forward to the trip.
2 What would you like to know?
3 Don't forget to take your umbrella.

b Complete these sentences about yourself. In pairs, practice saying your sentences.

1 I'm looking forward to ...
2 I'd like to know ...

4 **Reading and speaking**

a Bill Bryson is a very successful American author. Read this extract about his first visit to Britain and mark the sentences T (true) or F (false).

I was completely ignorant about many things in Britain. I found that British beer was warm. Before I bought my beer, I sat for half an hour in a pub (a kind of bar) before I realized you had to order at the bar. I then tried the same thing in a tea-room and was told to sit down. The tea-room lady called me "love" and most of the men called me "mate." British people didn't eat with a fork like Americans but used a knife and fork. I had never had tea with milk in it before or had my main meal at 7 o'clock in the evening. British cars drove on the left! Among the many terms new to me were *loo* (bathroom), *semi-detached house* (a building divided into two houses) and *au pair* (a foreign girl who works for a family).

According to Bill Bryson:

1 British beer is served cold.   T ◯   F ◯

2 In English pubs a member of the staff serves you at your table.   T ◯   F ◯

3 Many women call people "love."   T ◯   F ◯

4 English people eat in the same way as Americans.   T ◯   F ◯

5 The writer normally drank tea without milk.   T ◯   F ◯

6 The biggest meal in Britain is lunch.   T ◯   F ◯

7 In the U.S. they drive on the right.   T ◯   F ◯

8 *Loo* in British English means bathroom in American English.   T ◯   F ◯

b Imagine a British tourist is visiting your country. What would he or she find different about customs in your country? In groups, discuss what to tell the tourist.

Remember to drive on the right in our country. You drive on the left!

4 Lifeline to intercultural communication

1 Speaking and listening

a **In pairs, look at the photographs. Answer the questions with your opinions.**

1 Are the people family, friends or business colleagues?

2 Are the places in the photographs formal or informal? Are the people acting in a formal or informal manner?

b **Listen to the conversation. Then answer the questions in the table.**

	Photograph A	Photograph B
1 Are the people family, friends or colleagues?		
2 Are the occasions formal or informal?		
3 What are the occasions?		
4 In what month was each event?		
5 Why did Jerry enjoy the two events?		

c **Listen again and check your answers.**

2 Speaking

In groups, consider the situations in the photographs in exercise 1. Would the situations be similar in your country, or do you have very different customs?

Photograph A:

1 The company president is eating with some young employees from the warehouse.

2 Men and women are preparing food together.

3 Many people have brought their children to the picnic.

Photograph B:

1 The anniversary dinner is from 7–10 p.m. There isn't a party after the dinner.

2 People are talking and laughing. They look very relaxed.

3 Speaking and reading

a How much do you know about customs in English-speaking countries? In pairs, complete the quiz.

Cultural Competence Quiz

Imagine you are living in an English-speaking country.
For each of the following situations, what would be the most culturally appropriate thing to do?

1 You are invited to a dinner party at 8:00 p.m. You should arrive ...
a) at about 7:30   b) at about 8:00   c) at about 8:30

2 You have a business appointment at 2:00. You should arrive ...
a) at about 1:30   b) at about 1:45   c) at 2:00–2:10

3 You are at a business party and you want to introduce a person to a colleague. Suddenly, you can't remember the person's last name. What do you do?
a) Say to the colleague simply, "This is John."   b) Say to John, "I'm sorry but I've forgotton your last name."   c) Say "This is my colleague."

4 You are eating dinner at someone's house. The host offers you more of a chicken dish you didn't like very much. What's the best thing to say?
a) "No, thank you, but I'd love some more salad."   b) "No, thank you. I'm allergic to to chicken."   c) "Yes, please." (and eat it anyway)

5 You are visiting a friend and you want to smoke. What should you do?
a) offer him/her a cigarette and begin to smoke   b) not smoke   c) ask if it's OK to smoke

6 You are introduced to a woman in an informal situation. You should ...
a) kiss her lips   b) kiss her hand   c) say "It's nice to meet you."

7 You are introduced to a woman in a business situation. You should ...
a) kiss her cheek   b) shake hands   c) say "Cheers."

8 You go out to dinner with friends. There are both men and women in the group. Who will probably pay the bill?
a) everyone in the group   b) the men   c) the women

Check your cultural competence.

1 b	5 c	1–2: You need a cultural competence class!
2 b	6 c	3–4: You're not very culturally competent.
3 b	7 b	5–6: You've got a good idea about English-speaking cultures.
4 a	8 a	7–8: You're ready to travel!

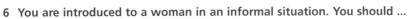

b In pairs, complete the quiz in relation to your culture. How many answers are the same as for English-speaking cultures? How many are different?

Unit 8 Good health

1 You and your body

1 Reading and speaking

a How well do you think you know your body? Choose one option. Take a class survey. How many people chose each option?

1 I'm not a doctor, but I think I know a lot about how my body works.

2 I know a little about my body, but there's a lot I don't know.

3 I don't think I know very much at all about how my body works.

b Now take this quiz about the human body. Mark each statement T (true) or F (false).

BODY QUIZ

1 The left side of your brain controls the left side of your body. ○

2 You have approximately 96,558 km. of blood vessels in your body. ○

3 It takes eight minutes for your blood to flow from your heart to your big toe and back. ○

4 When you rest, your heart beats from 60 to 80 times per minute. ○

5 Your body replaces the top layer of skin every 15–20 days. ○

6 About one quarter of your bones are in your feet. ○

7 When you have a bad cold, food doesn't taste good because your sense of taste is affected. ○

8 When you move, your body uses units of energy called calories. ○

9 To keep healthy, you need to eat about the same number of calories as you burn. ○

10 To burn the calories taken in when you eat a chocolate bar, you have to walk fast for about 20 minutes. ○

11 You don't burn any calories when you sit and read. ○

12 About two thirds of your body consists of water. ○

c In groups, compare your answers. Try to give reasons for your answers.

d Now check the answers to the quiz. Look at the options in part a again.
Would you choose a different option now?

Answers to quiz:
1 F: The left side of the brain controls the right side of the body, and vice versa.
2 T
3 F: It takes less than one minute.
4 T
5 T
6 T
7 F: Your sense of *smell* is affected, and you have to be able to smell to taste things.
8 T
9 T: Too many calories and you get fat; too few and you won't have enough energy.
10 F: You have to walk fast for more than two hours to burn those 400 calories!
11 F: You burn 60–80 calories per hour.
12 T

Score:
10–12: You know a lot about how your body works!
6–9: You know a little about your body.
1–5: You don't know very much about your body!

2 Speaking, listening and writing

a In pairs, discuss these questions.

1 What are the benefits of regular exercise?

2 Is age a limitation for doing exercise?

3 What kind of exercise do you usually do?

b Listen to the interview and see how many benefits
you thought of. How many of these facts
didn't you know before?

c Listen again. Then complete the sentences in a
logical way using information from the interview.
Complete questions 5 and 6 with your own ideas.

1 It isn't necessary to ...

2 If you exercise three times a week, ...

3 You should always ...

4 It isn't a good idea to ...

5 I think ...

6 In my opinion, ...

3 Speaking

In groups, discuss your ideas about exercise.

1 How many of the things mentioned in the interview in exercise 2 do you do?

2 What don't you do?

3 What will you change now?

2 Dangerous practices

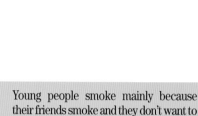

1 Speaking and reading

a **In groups, discuss these questions.**

1   Why do people smoke?
2   What are the problems associated with smoking?
3   In your country, which age group smokes the most – teenagers, young adults or older adults?
4   Is smoking increasing or decreasing in your country?
5   How are cigarettes usually advertised in your country?

b **Read the text and compare the ideas with your answers in part a.**

SMOKING
A DANGEROUS PRACTICE

Some illnesses are self-inflicted. Smoking, for instance, has been directly linked to 24 diseases including lung cancer and cardio-vascular problems. Every year 4 million people  in the world die of smoking-related illnesses. That figure is expected to rise to about 10 million by 2030. In the U.S., $60 billion is spent every year on treatment of people with conditions directly caused by smoking cigarettes.

Why smoke?
Why do people smoke? Partly because of the effects of advertising which promotes smoking as something sophisticated and fashionable.

Young people smoke mainly because their friends smoke and they don't want to be different. Children of smokers tend to smoke as well.

Anti-smoking campaigns
Tobacco used to be very fashionable, but now many people realize that it really is bad for you – smoking can shorten your life by five to eight years. One of the first anti-smoking campaigners was Britain's King James I (1603 to 1625). He had leaflets printed to tell people that it was a dangerous habit. There are now anti-smoking groups everywhere in the world. If you care about people's health, join one now!

Smoking – face the facts!

Number of deaths every
year as a result of smoking: . . . .
Estimated deaths caused by smoking in 2030: . . . .
Annual cost of treatment in U.S.
for smoking-related illnesses: . . . .
Main reasons people start to smoke: . . . .
Effects of smoking: . . . .
First anti-smoking campaign: . . . .

c **Read the text again and complete the fact sheet.**

2 Grammar builder: causatives *have / get* something done

a **Look at the rules. Then make sentences using *have / get* something done with the following prompts.**
We frequently use *have / get* something *done* to describe a service done for us by someone.

have / get	+ object	+ past participle
get	**your chest**	**x-rayed**
have	**your lungs**	**checked**

1 She / get / hair / cut last weekend.
2 I / have / my car / repair at the moment.
3 They / have / house / paint by an interior designer.
4 If you have headaches, you should get / your eyes / test.
5 We / have / the food / prepare by a catering company.

b **In groups, talk about things you want to have / get done in the near future.**

I want to have my hair cut on the weekend.

3 Writing and speaking

a **Read the e-mail from a friend. You know that he/she is a heavy smoker.**
Write an e-mail trying to persuade him/her to give up.
Use ideas from the boxes below or your own ideas.

```
Hi!
Thanks for your e-mail. I'm OK I guess, but I'm not feeling very well. I cough a lot and I
always feel tired. I don't know what's wrong - I must have the flu or something. Anyway,
let me know what you're doing this weekend ...
```

Get medical advice.

See your doctor.   Get your chest x-rayed.   Have your lungs checked.

Evaluate your smoking habits.
Why do you smoke?   When do you smoke?   Where do you smoke?

Choose a strategy.
Tell people you're giving up smoking.   Get acupuncture.
Remove temptation – ashtrays, cigarettes.   Cut down on smoking gradually.
Chew nicotine gum.   Cut out cigarettes completely.

b **In groups, talk about the ideas in your e-mails.**

1 In your opinion, what are the best ways to stop smoking?
2 Has anyone in your group stopped smoking?
3 How did they do it?

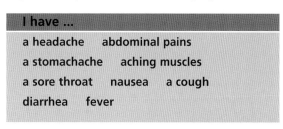

3 The best remedies

1 Word builder: health problems

a In pairs, complete the table with symptoms from the boxes below.

I have ...
a headache   abdominal pains
a stomachache   aching muscles
a sore throat   nausea   a cough
diarrhea   fever

I'm ...
tired   sneezing

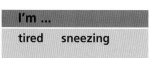

Illness	Symptoms	Remedies
the flu (influenza)		
a cold		
food poisoning		
appendicitis		
a migraine		

b Then write remedies for the illnesses in the second column.

Take antibiotics	Eat fruit and vegetables	Eat very little food
Take a decongestant	Drink fluids	Take aspirin
Drink herbal tea	Rest in bed	Have surgery

c Have you ever had any of these illnesses? What did you do?

2 Reading and writing

Read and write the illnesses from exercise 1 in the spaces.

If you have a stomachache, nausea and diarrhea, you may have (1) .... Rest in bed, drink herbal tea and don't eat very much. If the symptoms continue, see your doctor. You may need some antibiotics.

The symptoms of (2) .... are often nausea, fever and abdominal pains, especially on the right side. See a doctor immediately because you may need surgery!

(3) .... is a virus, so antibiotics won't help. The symptoms are aching muscles, headache, fever and sometimes sneezing. Rest in bed, drink fluids and take aspirin.

(4) .... is similar to influenza, but usually less severe. The symptoms are usually sneezing, coughing, headache and sometimes fever. Take aspirin, and if necessary, a decongestant.

(5) .... is a type of headache, but there are usually other symptoms. You may have nausea and vision problems, and you may be extremely sensitive to light and noise.

3 Listening

a Listen and choose the correct answer.

1 Jim is   a) sick ◯   b) tired ◯   c) hungry ◯

2 Connie is probably   a) Jim's wife ◯   b) Jim's doctor ◯   c) Jim's boss ◯

b Listen again and answer the questions.

1 What does Jim think he has?

2 What are his symptoms?

3 What does Connie think he might have?

4 What does she say he should do?

4 Grammar builder: *must, may/might, can't*

a Look at this conversation. Answer the questions.

A: *I have a stomachache. I **might** have appendicitis.*

B: *You **can't** have appendicitis because you don't have fever. It **may** be something you ate.*

A: *If I'm not better tomorrow, then it **must** be appendicitis.*

1 Which of the words in bold express strong probability?

2 Which of the words express possibility?

3 Which two words have the same meaning?

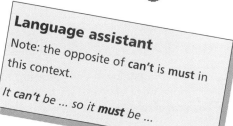

Language assistant

Note: the opposite of **can't** is **must** in this context.

*It **can't** be ... so it **must** be ...*

b Complete the sentences using *must, may / might,* or *can't.*

1 My arms ache. It .... be the tennis match I played yesterday. I played for four hours!

2 John told me to eat a lot of meat, but that .... be right. A lot of meat isn't good for you.

3 You .... have a migraine. I'm not sure.

4 I can't sleep at night. It .... be the coffee I'm drinking, or maybe I'm stressed.

5 Speaking

Work in pairs. Student A, you are a doctor. Student B, you are a patient. Then change roles.

Patient	Doctor
Say how you feel (awful, terrible, etc.). →	Ask what's wrong.
Tell one of your symptoms. → ←	Ask about other symptoms.
Ask what the problem is. → ←	Say what you think the problem is.
Ask what you should do. → ←	Give advice.

4 Lifeline to alternative medicine

1 Speaking, writing and listening

a What do you know about each of these treatments? Write a list of any points you know.

> chiropractic   acupuncture   homeopathy

b Now listen to an interview with a homeopathic practitioner and complete the information.

Developed by a .... in ....

Introduced into U.S. in ....

By the end of the 19th century, ... % of American doctors were homeopathic practictioners.

Homeopathy: an alternative form of medical treatment based on two main principles:

1 ....

2 ....

Number of people using homeopathy in the U.S.: ....

Homeopathic remedies are useful for asthma, allergies, ... and ....

c Find out if anyone in your class has had homeopathic, chiropractic or acupuncture treatment.
Ask them to talk about their experience.

2 Reading and writing

a In pairs, write two questions you would like to ask about acupuncture and chiropractic.

b Read the articles quickly to see if they answer your questions.

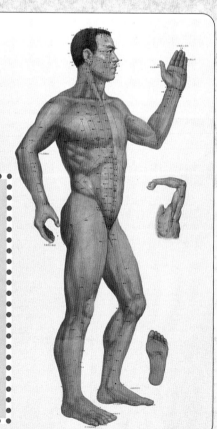

Acupuncture is a traditional Chinese medicine dating from 200-100 B.C. It is based on the theory that the body has an energy force or "Qi" (chi) which influences your health. The Qi travels through 14 meridians (or channels) in the body. At the points where these meridians come near the surface of the skin, thin, sharp needles are used to puncture the skin and restore the balance of energy. Acupuncturists usually use needles but may also use heat, pressure, friction, suction or impulses of electromagnetic energy to stimulate the acupuncture points. People have acupuncture done for many things, including chronic pain, drug addiction, arthritis, chemotherapy-induced nausea and mental illness.

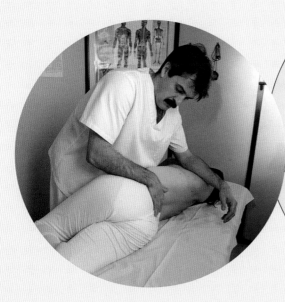

The field of chiropractic was founded by David Daniel Palmer in the 1890s. He believed that partial dislocation of the vertebrae could cause illness. By adjusting the vertebrae, the patient's health could be restored. Chiropractic comes from the Greek words for "hand" (cheiros) and "done by" (praktos) meaning "done by hand." The basic technique in chiropractic is manipulating and adjusting bone and tissue, particularly in the spinal column. Chiropractors use a variety of manual, mechanical and electrical treatments. They provide drug-free, non-surgical management of back and neck pain as well as headaches. The prevention of illness and the promotion of good health through proper diet, exercise and lifestyle are other important features of chiropractic medicine.

c In groups, underline all the medical words in the articles. Try to work out the meanings of any new words.

acupuncture   meridian

d Now match the list of words with the definitions.

1 needle .....   2 therapeutic .....   3 ailment .....   4 manual .....   5 drug .....   6 proper .....

a) beneficial   b) illness   c) medicine   d) small, very thin piece of metal   e) correct   f) by hand

3 Pronunciation: word stress

a Listen to these words. Then write them in the correct column according to their stress.

acupuncture   meridian   stimulate   adjust   energy   addiction   technique   medicine

stress on the first syllable	stress on the second syllable
acupuncture	meridian

b Listen and check.

c In pairs, look back at the articles in exercise 2. Find two more words for each column.

d Practice saying the words in each column.

4 Speaking

In groups, look at these sayings about health. Are they based on truth or myth?
Do you know any sayings about health in your language?

An apple a day keeps the doctor away.

Feed a cold, starve a fever.

Early to bed and early to rise makes a man healthy, wealthy and wise.

Checkpoint 4

1 Check your progress

a Complete the conversation using the correct form of the word in parentheses.

Jack: Is that a crocodile skin bag, Jill?

Jill: No, Jack. This bag (1) .... (*make*) of plastic.

Jack: Good. Too many wild animal skins (2) .... (*use*) to make clothes and things.

Jill: I agree. But this bag is nice, isn't it?

Jack: Yes, it is. I'd like (3) .... (*buy*) one for Sue's birthday.

Jill: Well, they (4) .... (*sell*) them in Howard's on Tenth Avenue at the moment.

Jack: Thanks. Oh, are you coming to Sue's birthday party on Saturday?

Jill: Of course. I'm looking forward to (5) .... (*see*) her again. We haven't met for months.

Jack: Don't forget (6) .... (*bring*) your guitar. We always enjoy (7) .... (*listen*) to you sing.

Jill: Well, you must (8) .... (*be*) masochists!

Jack: No – you're good, Jill. You should enter a talent contest.

Jill: No way, Jack. I'll never get used to (9) .... (*perform*) in public. Well, I have to go. I'm going to get my car (10) .... (*repair*). See you on Saturday!

b Complete the second sentence so that it means the same as the first.

11 It's almost certain that you have appendicitis – all the symptoms are right.

You .... appendicitis – all the symptoms are right.

12 It's difficult for me to get up early in the morning.

I have trouble .... in the morning.

13 All sorts of people use the Internet now.

The Internet .... now.

14 I don't believe he's British – he has a strong American accent.

He .... British – he has a strong American accent.

15 Somebody is going to paint their house for them.

They're going to ....

Score out of 20

○ 18–20 Excellent! ○ 15–17 Very good! ○ 12–14 OK, but review. ○ 9–11 You have some problems. Review units 7 and 8. ○ 0–8 Talk to your teacher.

2 Games to play

a In teams, play this culture quiz. There is one point for the correct information, and one point for correct English.

Give the country where the following are typically eaten, drunk, danced, played / sung, spoken or worn.

1   Dance – the tango

2   Clothes – kimonos

3   Music – reggae

4   Food – roast beef

5   Language – Dutch

6   Drink – ouzo

7   Music – the fado

8   Food – paella

9   Language – Guaraní

10   Clothes – kilts

11   Drink – sake

12   Dance – the samba

Food – sushi

Sushi is eaten in Japan.

b Be prepared! The teacher might produce another list for a second competition.

3 My world

Birthdays are celebrated almost everywhere in the world, but customs differ from country to country, family to family, and even person to person. In groups, discuss these questions.

1   How are birthdays usually celebrated in your family?

2   How do you like to celebrate your own birthday?

4 Personal word bank

a Complete the labels for the illustration.

b Now check your labels using the words in the box.

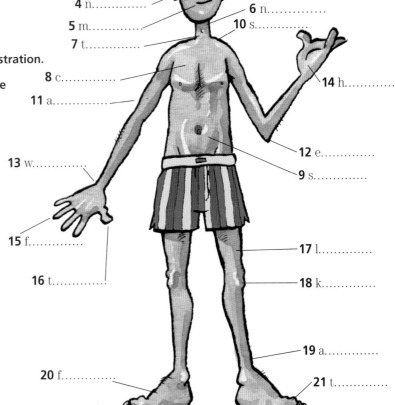

1 h.............

2 e.............

3 e.............

4 n.............

5 m.............

6 n.............

7 t.............

8 c.............

9 s.............

10 s.............

11 a.............

12 e.............

13 w.............

14 h.............

15 f.............

16 t.............

17 l.............

18 k.............

19 a.............

20 f.............

21 t.............

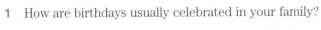

1 head	**12** elbow
2 eye	**13** wrist
3 ear	**14** hand
4 nose	**15** finger
5 mouth	**16** thumb
6 neck	**17** leg
7 throat	**18** knee
8 chest	**19** ankle
9 stomach	**20** foot
10 shoulder	**21** toe
11 arm	

Unit 9 Imagination

1 Dreams

1 Reading and speaking

a Read this extract from a poem, and look at the photographs. What do you know about these people?

> We are the music-makers,
> And we are the dreamers of dreams,
> ...
> Yet we are the movers and shakers
> Of the world for ever, it seems.

b Match each of these statements with one of the people in the photographs.

1 "I wish I were as close as this to all the poor people in the world."

2 "I have a dream that one day this nation will rise up and live out the true meaning of its creed – that all men are created equal."

3 "I hope my music will bring English and Spanish speakers together."

4 "That's one small step for man, one giant leap for mankind."

c Who are the creative people who "move and shake" your country or the world today? Discuss in pairs or groups.

2 Word builder: words with similar meanings – *wish / hope / expect / wait*

a Match these sentences with their meanings.

1 I wish I were as close as this to all the poor people in the world.

2 I hope my music will bring English and Spanish speakers together.

3 I'm waiting for the results of the examination.

4 I expect I'll pass the exam.

a) They sometimes take weeks or months.

b) I'm really confident about it.

c) But I'm not, just this crowd of people.

d) That's difficult, but perhaps music will do it.

b Now match the words with the definitions.

1 wait
2 expect
3 wish
4 hope

a) to believe or feel confident that something will happen
b) to desire something that is possible, but perhaps difficult
c) to let time pass until something happens, or until you can do something
d) to desire something which is contrary to reality, or improbable

3 Speaking and reading

a Answer these questions. Then read the article and check your answers.

1 Was Martin Luther King, Jr., a jazz musician, a church minister or a medical doctor?
2 Was racial segregation in public transportation in the U.S. prohibited in 1929, 1956 or 1965?
3 When and how did King die?

Dr. Martin Luther King, Jr., 1929 – 1968

Dr. Martin Luther King, Jr. was born in 1929, when racial discrimination was widespread in the U.S. He became a Baptist minister, and a civil rights leader. On August 28, 1963, he declared in a speech: "I have a dream today!" He believed it was possible for people of all races and religions in his country to live together in equality and harmony. He hoped to see that goal reached in his lifetime, but he did not expect it to happen by itself so he organized peaceful marches and boycotts.

The Supreme Court had already prohibited racial segregation in public transportation in 1956. In 1964, the Civil Rights Act was passed, and the Voting Rights Act in 1965, which allowed all adult Americans to vote.

Sadly, King did not live to see the process of integration completed. He was assassinated in 1968, a victim of the racial violence he wished to eradicate. His dream lives on at the beginning of this new millennium but it is still partly a dream, not totally reality.

b Read the article again and answer the questions.

1 What was still a big problem in the U.S. in 1929?
2 Why did Martin Luther King organize marches?
3 What did the Voting Rights Act achieve?
4 How did Martin Luther King die?
5 Is racial harmony a reality today?

4 Writing and speaking

a Write some of your dreams.

I want to travel around India.
I would like to see ...

b In groups, talk about your dreams.

A: *I want to travel around India.*
B: *Why do you want to go there?*
A: *I want to eat real Indian food and I want to see ...*

2 Wishes and hopes

1 Listening and speaking

a Listen to two friends talking, and look at the list below. Decide which things are facts (F) and which are wishes (W) about Lucy's life.

		F	W
Job:	interesting and well-paid	○	○
Courses of study:	interesting and challenging	○	○
Neighborhood:	clean and quiet	○	○
Family:	living very close to Lucy	○	○

b Listen again and answer the questions.

1 Does Lucy enjoy her job?
2 Does Lucy live in the country or in a city?
3 Does Lucy live near the west coast?
4 In general, do you think Lucy's life is going better or worse than Frank's?

2 Grammar builder: wishes about the present, hopes for the future

a Look at these sentences. In pairs, answer the questions.

*I wish I **spoke** perfect French.*
*They all wish the weather **were** warmer.*
*I wish those courses **were** as interesting and*
challenging as my job.
*I wish I **lived** in a cleaner, quieter area.*
*I bet you wish you **could** visit them more often.*

1 What is the form of the verb after *wish*?
2 In combination with *wish*, does that form indicate that something is true or untrue?

> **Language assistant**
> After **wish** or **if**, for the singular verb *be* use **were** or **was**:
> *I wish I **were** richer.* / *I wish I **was** richer.*
> *If I **were** richer ...* / *If I **was** richer ...*
> In the expression **If I were you ...**, **were** is more common than **was**.

b Look at these sentences. What two different forms of verb can be used after *hope*?

1 I hope I **get** a good job when I graduate.
2 Sam hopes he**'ll win** the race.
3 I hope the winner **is** Sam.
4 I hope he**'ll be** first again this year.

c Complete these sentences with an appropriate form of *speak*, *know* or *learn*.

1 I wish I .... almost perfect English.
2 I hope I .... it quite fluently in the near future.
3 My father, who speaks excellent English, wishes he .... more about computers.
4 He hopes he .... much more about them now that he has one at home.

3 Speaking

In groups, discuss things you
wish were different.
Use a topic from the box.

Free time
The environment
My house
The city

A: *I wish there were less
traffic in our city.*

B: *Yes, I agree. I hope they
improve the public
transportation soon.*

A: *I wish I had more
opportunities to practice
English.*

B: *So do I. I'd like to get
cable TV and listen to
more English.*

4 Writing and reading

a Write a list of wishes and hopes.
Use this poem outline to help you.

*Life is too good to complain,
But I wish ...
And I hope ...
I wish ...
And I hope ...
But let's enjoy the sun and the rain,
For life is too good to complain.*

b Now read your poem to the class and vote for the best one.

3 Creatures of the imagination

1 Reading and speaking

a In groups, say what you know about these monsters.

b Read the brief biographies below and complete these notes.

Mary Shelley

Born in (1) ...., England, in (2) ....

Ran away with the poet (3) .... in (4) ....,

and married him in (5) .... Began the novel

(6) .... in (7) ...., and published it in

(8) .... Died in (9) ....

Bram Stoker

Born in (10) ...., Ireland, in (11) .... Studied at (12) ....,

and worked as (13) .... and .... Moved to (14) ...., and

worked for the well-known (15) ...., Sir Henry Irving. Published the novel

(16) .... in (17) .... Died in (18) ....

Mary Wollstonecraft Shelley (1797-1851) was born in London. At the age of 16, Mary ran away to France with the poet Percy Bysshe Shelley, who was already married at that time. They married three years later, after the death of Shelley's first wife.

The Shelleys spent the summer of 1816 in Switzerland with another English poet, Lord Byron. To pass the time, they all wrote ghost stories or horror stories, and that is when Mary began *Frankenstein*. It was published in 1818.

In that same year, the Shelleys moved to Italy, where Shelley died in 1822 at the age of 30. In 1823, Mary returned to England with her son. She wrote many other stories, but nothing compared with her original and impressive tale of Frankenstein and the creature he brought to life. It's still a very popular story today and several *Frankenstein* movies have been made.

Abraham (Bram) Stoker (1847-1912) was born in Dublin. He studied at Trinity College. After working for several years in Dublin as a civil servant and journalist, he moved to London, where he became personal manager to the most famous actor of the time, Henry Irving. He wrote many works of fiction, but his name is remembered only for *Dracula*, published in 1897. It soon became a classic and remains so today and many famous *Dracula* movies have been made.

c Have you seen the movies or read the books of *Dracula* and *Frankenstein*? Which did you prefer?

2 Grammar builder: the second conditional

a Look at these sentences. Underline *if* and the verbs.

1 If Dracula really existed, we would all be in danger at night.
2 I would always keep a cross and some garlic with me if I believed in Dracula.
3 If I met a monster like Dracula, I'd faint on the spot.
4 If I were Dracula, I'd open a blood donor center.

b In pairs, answer the questions.

1 Are the sentences in part a about real situations or imaginary ones?
2 Is *if* always at the beginning of the sentence?
3 What form of the verb is used after *if*?
4 What form of the verb is used in the other half of the sentence?
5 What is the complete form for *'d* as in *I'd*?

c Complete these sentences with your own ideas. In pairs, compare your completed sentences.

1 If I had a castle in Transylvania, I ...
2 If I .... Madonna at a party, I ...
3 **A:** What .... you do if you .... ten million dollars in a lottery?
   B: I ...
4 If I found $100 under a restaurant table, I ...

3 Pronunciation: sentence stress – second conditional

a Look at these sentences. Listen and underline the words with strong stress or emphasis.

1 If <u>I</u> were <u>you</u>, <u>I'd</u> say <u>no</u>.
2 I'd go back to college if I lost my job.
3 If I were President, I'd reduce taxes.
4 What would you do if you saw a ghost?

b Listen again, and repeat the sentences.

4 Speaking

In groups, look back at your ideas in exercise 2c and compare your ideas.

A: What would you do if you had a castle in Transylvania?
B: I'd ...

4 Lifeline to physical sciences

1 Speaking and listening

a In pairs or groups, say what you know about this famous person. If you know nothing, what can you guess from the photograph?

b Look at the biographical notes. Can you guess any of the missing information?

STEPHEN WILLIAM HAWKING

Born January 8, (1) .... – exactly (2) .... years after the death of Galileo.

Studied (3) .... at the University of (4) ....

Suffers from ALS, an incurable disease of the (5) .... system.

Communicates through a (6) .... and speech-synthesizer.

Published the scientific best-seller, *A Brief* (7) .... in (8) ....

Influential work on (9) .... holes, and on the (10) .... and future of the universe.

---

c Now listen to part of a radio talk about Stephen Hawking, and complete the notes.

2 Reading and speaking

a Look at the two diagrams and decide which is correct.

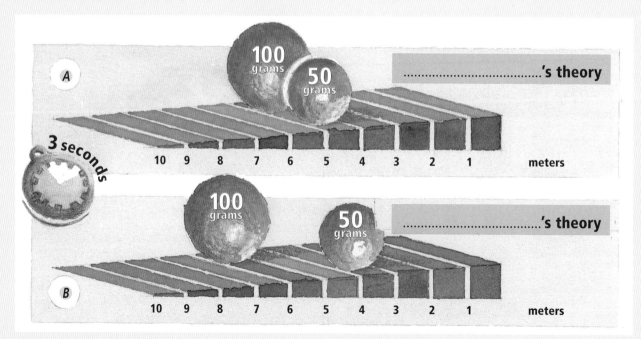

b Read the extract, check your answer to
part a, and write the names "Aristotle"
and "Galileo" in the appropriate
space on the diagrams on page 84.

c Mark these statements T (true)
or F (false). Then discuss your
answers in pairs or groups.

1 Aristotle believed that checking
theories was essential.   T ◯ F ◯

2 Galileo pioneered scientific
observation.   T ◯ F ◯

3 Galileo dropped weights from
the Tower of Pisa to check the
speed of falling objects.   T ◯ F ◯

4 Galileo showed that the speed
of falling objects constantly
increases.   T ◯ F ◯

5 The weight of an object
determines how fast it falls. T ◯ F ◯

Our present ideas about movement date back to
Galileo and Newton. Before them people
believed Aristotle, who said that the natural state
of an object was to be at rest and that it moved
only if driven by a force or impulse. He thought
that a heavy object should fall faster than a light
one, because it would have a greater pull toward
the earth. At that time, nobody checked theories
by observation, so no one tried to see whether
objects of different weight did in fact fall at
different speeds.

Until Galileo. The story is that Galileo
demonstrated that Aristotle's theory was false by
dropping weights from the Leaning Tower of
Pisa! That's probably not true, but he did roll
balls of different weights down a smooth slope.
The situation is similar to that of heavy objects
falling vertically, but it is easier to observe
because the objects don't move so fast. Galileo's
measurements showed that each ball increased its
speed at the same rate, no matter what its weight.
For example, if you let go of a ball on a slope that
drops one meter for every ten meters you go
along it, the ball will be traveling down the slope
at a speed of about one meter per second after one
meter, two meters per second after two seconds,
and so on, however heavy the ball.

7

3 Speaking

What do you know about science? In teams, answer these questions to find out.

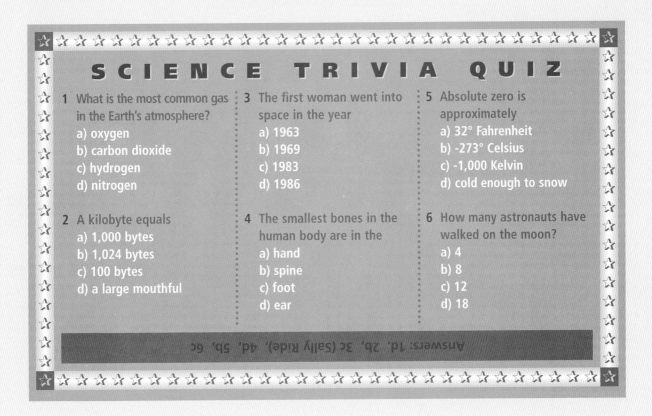

SCIENCE TRIVIA QUIZ

1 What is the most common gas
in the Earth's atmosphere?
a) oxygen
b) carbon dioxide
c) hydrogen
d) nitrogen

2 A kilobyte equals
a) 1,000 bytes
b) 1,024 bytes
c) 100 bytes
d) a large mouthful

3 The first woman went into
space in the year
a) 1963
b) 1969
c) 1983
d) 1986

4 The smallest bones in the
human body are in the
a) hand
b) spine
c) foot
d) ear

5 Absolute zero is
approximately
a) 32° Fahrenheit
b) -273° Celsius
c) -1,000 Kelvin
d) cold enough to snow

6 How many astronauts have
walked on the moon?
a) 4
b) 8
c) 12
d) 18

Answers: 1d, 2b, 3c (Sally Ride), 4d, 5b, 6c

Unit 10 Seeing the world

maps   travel books

VR   travel videos

Armchair travel

1 Listening and speaking

a Imagine the bookstore of the future. What would you be interested in if you were in that store?

b Listen to two people talking in the store.

1 Why are they there?

2 What places are they interested in?

	Judy	Peter
Reasons for being in the store		
Places they are interested in		

c Listen again and compare your notes with another student.

2 Speaking

a Look at the table. Check (✓) your attitude toward the different options for "armchair travel," and if you have used them or not. In groups, compare and discuss your completed tables.

A: I don't like studying maps, but I have used them.

B: I like studying maps, but I don't like reading travel books.

	Like	Not sure	Don't like	Used	Not used
Studying maps					
Reading travel books					
Watching videos or TV documentaries					
Talking to friends about their trips					
Making a "virtual" trip					

b If you could go on a "virtual" trip, where would you go? Why?

I would go to Africa because I'd like to see all the animals there.

3 Reading and speaking

In pairs, read the profiles and travel guides and agree on a vacation destination for Bill and Jane.

WONDERWORLD HOLIDAYS Inc.

Wonderworld Holidays Inc.
Wonderworld House, 435 Main Street, Seattle WA 98117
Telephone: (123) 482-2193 Fax. (123) 482-2194

BIG WONDER COMPETITION

Dear Prizewinner!

Congratulations! You aren't going to be an armchair traveler any more. You've won a vacation for two people and have three choices of destination.

Sincerely,

Competition Manager

Sydney

Enjoy the sun, sea and sand in beautiful Sydney. See the amazing Sydney Harbour Bridge and visit the stunning Opera House. Then relax on Bondi Beach and decide where you want to spend the evening – you have a fantastic choice of nightspots, and there's always lots of wonderful food.

Ibiza

Come for a relaxing, sunny vacation to the party capital, Ibiza. We have lots of sun, lots of great beaches and lots of bars and nightclubs. Dance all night and lie on the beach all day!

Your profile

Name: Bill
Profile: I enjoy sunbathing and going out in the evening. I love good food and want a relaxing vacation.

Your friend's profile

Name: Jane
Profile: She's an architect and loves architecture and going to museums. She loves good food and the sun.

Rome

The city for everybody who loves good food! Sit on the terrace and enjoy watching the people while eating wonderful pasta, pizza and ice cream. Spend the rest of your day exploring the history of Rome – the Colosseum, the Pantheon and a whole range of wonderful churches and palaces.

4 Writing

a Write a vacation profile for you.

b In pairs, choose the perfect destination for your partner.

The real thing

1 Reading and speaking

a In pairs or groups, discuss a trip each of you has made in your own country or abroad.
Use the questions in the box to help you.

Where did you go?
Why did you go?
How did you travel – by bus, train, car, plane, or some other means of transportation?
Did you enjoy the trip? Why? / Why not?

b Read the article and complete the notes.

First passenger train service: (1) ...1825...

First bus service: (2) ....

First passenger jet plane service: (3) ....

First jumbo jet service: (4) ....

World's busiest airport: (5) ....–

(6) .... passengers a day,

(7) .... a year. World's busiest

international airport: (8) .... –

(9) .... passengers a year,

(10) .... different airlines.

c In groups, discuss these questions.

1 Have you ever traveled by air?

2 What are the most common forms of transportation in your country?

3 What are the advantages and disadvantages of each?

4 How do you prefer to travel?

GETTING THERE

Mass passenger transportation really began with trains (1825) and buses (1895). Both kinds of transportation have changed a lot over the years and there are now high-speed trains which get you to your destination much quicker – the TGV in France, the Bullet Train in Japan and ICE in Germany, for example.

Buses and trains continue to provide a means of transportation for most people in the world.

The other type of mass transportation is, of course, the airplane. Airplanes have been used for taking passengers for only the last 50 years. Jet planes were first used for passengers in 1952, and in 1970 jumbo jets were introduced. They allowed enormous numbers of people to fly from country to country and continent to continent fast, safely and relatively cheaply.

The numbers of passengers now are impressive. Chicago's O'Hare Airport claims that it is the busiest in the world, moving almost 200,000 passengers a day, over 70 million a year. The management of London's Heathrow Airport says it moves the most *international* passengers (many of O'Hare's passengers are on domestic flights), with over 60 million a year on more than 90 different airlines. But Chicago and London are closely followed by Atlanta, Paris and hundreds of other airports around the world. How will transportation change in the next 50 years?

2 Grammar builder: reporting statements and opinions

a Look at these sentences with reporting verbs.

*My friend **tells** me there's a cheap flight on Mondays.*
*He **thinks** it leaves at 7:00 a.m.*

Look back at the article on page 88 and find two more examples of reporting verbs.

> **Language assistant**
> The two parts of each sentence (*My friend tells me / there's a cheap flight on Mondays.*) can be connected with the word **that** (*My friend tells me that there's a cheap flight on Mondays.*) but it is usually omitted, especially in informal speech.

b Complete these sentences using reporting verbs from the box. There may be more than one possible option.

believe	claim	say	tell	think

1 My brother lives in Bangkok. He .... me real Thai food is fantastic.
2 Hundreds of cities around the world .... they are more hospitable than any other.
3 Personally, I .... my own city is the most hospitable in the world. Am I prejudiced?
4 They .... travel broadens the mind.
5 Experts .... tourism will continue to grow.

3 Speaking

a Ask a partner about a city he/she knows where tourism is very important, and complete the table. It may be in your own country or abroad. Use the questions in the box to help you.

What's the name of the city?	What's your impression of the people?	Are things expensive or cheap there?

Name of city:	
Impressions of people:	
city:	
food:	
other, e.g. prices, weather:	

b In groups, report what you found out.

Amanda says the people in San Salvador are very friendly. She thinks ...

3 Visitors from abroad

1 Listening

a Listen to some tourists asking for information in London. Choose the correct answer.

1 The tourists are interested in
   a) shopping ○   **b)** nightlife ○
   c) places of interest / culture and history ○

2 The person they talk to is
   a) friendly and helpful ○   **b)** rude ○
   c) not interested ○

3 Madame Tussaud's is
   a) very far ○   **b)** a block ahead ○
   c) very near ○

4 The café is
   a) around the corner ○   **b)** on the left ○
   c) straight ahead ○

b Listen again. What do the tourists decide to do?

2 Reading

Use information from the guidebook to answer the tourist's questions.

1 Excuse me. Can you tell me how to get to Madame Tussaud's?
2 Can you tell me what time the museum closes?
3 Do you know when the museum started?
4 Do you know how many figures are in the museum?
5 What kinds of celebrities are represented in the museum?
6 How many people visit the museum each year?

MADAME TUSSAUD'S

Location: Marylebone Road, London NW1 5LR, one block from the Baker Street tube station
Opening times: Every day except Christmas day. Weekdays 10:00–5:00; weekends 9:30–5:30

History: Marie Grosholtz (1761-1850) was born in Strasbourg, and when her father died, her mother went to Berne to work for a doctor. He created anatomical figures from wax, and he taught Marie his art. She was very talented and soon began making wax figures of famous and important people. At the end of the 18th century, Marie married François Tussaud and became Madame Tussaud. The French economy was in decline after the French Revolution, so Madame Tussaud moved her exhibition of figures to England. The exhibition opened as a museum in 1835.

Today, there are over 400 figures in the museum, representing all types of celebrities. There are historical and political figures like the Royal Family and Gandhi, creative geniuses like Mozart and the Beatles, sports figures like Ayrton Senna and Muhammad Ali, actors like Cher and Mel Gibson, and society figures like Jerry Hall and Naomi Campbell. Over 2.5 million people per year visit Madame Tussaud's to see the incredibly life-like wax figures.

3 **Grammar builder:** requesting and stating information

a **Look at these sentences. What is the difference between the sentences in each pair?**

1   **a)** Where is Madame Tussaud's?

    b) Can you tell me where Madame Tussaud's is?

2   **a)** What time does it open?

    b) Could you tell me what time it opens?

3   **a)** Is there a café near here?

    b) Do you know if there's a café near here?

b **Now go back to exercise 2 and look at the requests for information. Are they direct or indirect questions?**

c **Complete these conversations.**

A: Can you tell me how much this guide book

     (1) ....?

B: Five pounds.

A: Oh. And how much (2) .... this one?

B: That one's four pounds.

A: (3) .... you sell T-shirts with a photo of Elvis?

B: Uh ... I'm not sure if we (4) .... that kind of thing. I'm new here.

A: Well, could you find out if (5) .... any T-shirts like that?

B: Sure, sure. I'll ask the manager.

4 **Pronunciation:** intonation – question forms

a **Listen to these sentences and mark the intonation.**

Do you know if there's a bank near here?

1   Can you tell me where the bank is?

2   What time is it?

3   Where's the bus stop?

4   Do you know which bus we need to take?

b **Listen again, and repeat the sentences.**

5 **Speaking**

In pairs, practice helping foreign visitors in your city. Student A, ask questions. Student B, answer Student A's questions.

Can you tell me where / when / how much ...?

Do you know what time / if ...?

4 Lifeline to tourism and hospitality

1 Speaking and listening

a Guess the missing facts.

b Listen and complete the information.

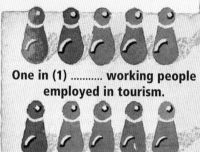

One in (1) .... working people employed in tourism.

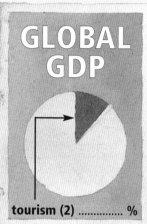

GLOBAL GDP

tourism (2) .... %

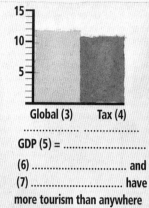

Global (3) .... Tax (4) ....

GDP (5) = ...

(6) .... and

(7) .... have more tourism than anywhere else in the world.

2 Reading and speaking

a Look at these photographs.

1 What do you know or imagine about the scenes?

2 Where are they?

3 Why do people go there?

Mardi Gras

Lord Upminster and friend, 1880

Cancún

Iguaçu Falls

Camino de Santiago, 12th century

Machu Picchu

b Read the summary from a chapter of a book on tourism and hospitality.
Match the numbered and underlined things with the photographs on page 92.

Summary

1 International tourism has a long history, going back to (1) medieval pilgrimages and (2) aristocratic "Grand Tours," but it has completely changed since World War II. There are two main reasons for this: the increased incomes and leisure time of the middle and lower classes in industrialized countries, and the dramatic advances in the speed and cost of long-distance transportation, particularly air transportation. International tourists now have the necessary money and time to travel abroad.

2 Tourist destinations vary. The most popular are still (3) beach resorts. However, the range of tourist attractions is enormous, including old cities and buildings, (4) archeological sites, museums and galleries, entertainment parks, safari parks, winter resorts, sports events, (5) natural sights and phenomena, cultural events, (6) festivals and shopping. One big decision for any place in tourist planning is whether to go for low-cost mass tourism or high-cost elite tourism. Key factors in the success of any tourist project are value for money, efficiency and hospitality. That last concept has become standard in naming the tourist industry: Tourism and Hospitality.

— 10 —

c In pairs, answer these questions.

1 Why has international tourism changed since World War II?
2 Look at the tourist destinations mentioned in paragraph 2.
Can you name an example of each in your country?
3 Why is the field of tourism referred to as Tourism and Hospitality?

3 Speaking and writing

a In pairs, discuss these questions.

1 What types of tourism are important in your country?
a) low-cost mass tourism b) high-cost elite tourism c) adventure or eco-tourism
2 Is tourism primarily domestic or foreign?
3 What special events or holidays increase tourism?
4 What are some of the problems with tourism in your country? How could they be solved?

b Work with another pair and write your ideas.

1 Check your progress

a Complete this text using words or phrases from the box. There are more words / phrases in the box than spaces in the text.

will	would	play	played	but	if	have	had	I'm	am I
	believe	hope	wish	says	tells				

Many people wish they (1) .... a musical instrument. But wishes don't make musicians.

You (2) .... never be a competent musician (3) .... you don't practice. And practice

is usually not enough – you need talent too. I don't really know if (4) .... talented or not,

because I've never taken music lessons. Still, we can all enjoy listening to good music.

I (5) .... I had more time to go to concerts, whether rock or classical. I (6) .... all

good music gives pleasure to people with open minds. I (7) .... I'll have more time in the

future, and more money, because concert tickets are usually very expensive. If I (8) ....

enough time and money, I (9) .... go to a concert every week. My sister (10) ....

me there's a good rock concert this Saturday, but I don't have enough money to go.

b Complete the second sentence so that it means the same as the first.

11 Barcelona is my ideal city, but unfortunately I don't live there.

I wish I .... – it's my ideal city.

12 Please don't let me get nervous in the interview!

I hope .... in the interview!

13 You could get a job in my company, but you don't speak English well enough.

If you .... English better, you .... a job in my company.

14 "New York – the greatest city in the world." (Ten million New Yorkers)

Ten million New Yorkers .... in the world.

15 Excuse me. Where's the Guggenheim Museum, please?

Excuse me. Can you tell me ....?

Score out of 20

| 18–20 Excellent! | 15–17 Very good! | 12–14 OK, but review. | 9–11 You have some problems. Review units 9 and 10. | 0–8 Talk to your teacher. |

2 Games to play

Read the instructions for "Whispers." Play the game.

- Teams sit or stand in lines from the back of the classroom to the front.

- Students at the back of each line, go to the front of the room.

- Look at the sentence the teacher shows (e.g. "I wish there was less traffic in our city" or "They say life is about the journey, not the destination").

- Students, go to the back of your line again and whisper the sentence to the student in front of you.

- Each student, whisper the sentence to the student in front.

- Student at the front of the line, go to the board and write the sentence.

- The first team with the correct sentence, or the best sentence when all teams have finished, wins a point.

- All move forward one place and repeat the game.

3 My world

In groups, talk about what you would do in the situations in the pictures.

A: Well, I'd probably …
B: So would I. But maybe …
C: If I were in that situation, …
D: Oh, no, I wouldn't do that. I'd …

4 Personal word bank

a Complete the table with tourist destinations in or out of your country.

Destination	Type of place	How to get there
Pompeii	archeological site	plane, bus / car

b In groups, compare your lists. Has anyone in the group been to any of the destinations? Ask them about their experiences.

Unit 11 Progress?

1 Early breakthroughs

1 Reading

a Read the definitions and decide which one refers to a discovery and which to an invention.

1 When someone finds out about something they did not know about before.

2 When someone creates something that has never been made or used before.

b Which of these things were inventions and which were discoveries?

1 fire 　　2 concrete 　　3 paper 　　4 gold

2 Reading and speaking

a In pairs, match the items in the photographs with the ancient civilizations you associate them with.

China	Egypt	Mesopotamia	Greece	Rome

b Read the passage to check your answers.

Ancient Inventors

Our world is to a large extent the result of things people invented. Imagine a world without textiles, concrete or paper! The people in ancient Mesopotamia invented the wheel in 3800 B.C. They also invented the sailboat and the world's first written laws.

The ancient Egyptians calculated a number system based on ten and invented a 365-day calendar and textiles to make clothes. They were also the first people to use cosmetics and perfumes as early as 4000 B.C. Both men and women painted their faces and cleaned their skin with oils and creams.

Ancient Greece invented the Olympic Games in 776 B.C., as well as trial by jury and democracy. The ancient Romans were more practical in their inventions. They developed concrete, paved roads and road signs.

The Chinese were prolific inventors and were responsible for inventing paper in about 100 A.D., and they invented gunpowder and the compass.

Finally, the flush toilet is not a modern invention at all. It is a product of the Minoan civilization in Crete and dates from about 2000 B.C.!

c Read the passage on page 96 again more carefully and complete the timeline of inventions.

B.C. 4000 .... 2000 .... 100 A.D.

cosmetics and perfumes | the wheel

d In pairs, decide which three inventions mentioned in the text were the most important and why. Compare your list with another pair.

3 Word builder: word formation

Complete the table with the correct forms of each word.

Verb	Noun for the activity	Noun for the person
invent		
	painting	
		cleaner
write		
		producer
	development	

4 Listening and speaking

a One of history's mysteries is why ancient people painted on the walls of caves. Why do you think they did these paintings? In pairs, make a list of possible reasons.

b Listen to a tourist guide talking about cave paintings. What reason for the paintings is mentioned?

c Listen again and mark the sentences T (true) or F (false).

1 Cave paintings exist on three different continents.   T ◯   F ◯

2 Cave painting started over 45,000 years ago.   T ◯   F ◯

3 Prehistoric artists worked in the dark.   T ◯   F ◯

4 They used four different colors.   T ◯   F ◯

5 They used their hands and brushes to paint.   T ◯   F ◯

6 The paintings were possibly part of a ritual.   T ◯   F ◯

7 Human figures were never painted.   T ◯   F ◯

2 Important inventions

1 Speaking

a In pairs, try to guess which items were invented in
which year.

aspirin	frozen food	compact disc
bicycle	microwave	
chewing gum	vulcanized rubber	

1816   1839   1848   1899   1924   1947   1972

b Can you think of any other modern inventions which are important?
With your partner, make a list. Compare your list with another pair.

2 Reading

a Look at the photographs. Do you associate any names with the objects?

b Read the extracts. Choose one extract and write notes to complete
the table on page 99.

THE SEWING MACHINE

There are many arguments about who really invented the sewing machine. There
were various machines made as early as 1755, and machines were made in
Europe and the U.S. during the 1700s and 1800s. However, most Americans
claim that the sewing machine was originally invented by Elias Howe, a farmer
from Massachusetts. He patented it in 1845, but he didn't sell any machines. He
tried to sell his machine in England, but he wasn't successful. When he returned
to the U.S., he found that many people were making his machines – and ignoring
his patent! One of those people was Isaac Singer, the name that is associated
today with sewing machines. After many lawsuits, Howe finally got his money,
but his name is not remembered.

THE RUBBER TIRE

In the 1830s, rubber was a new material. Everybody wanted things made of the
new waterproof gum from Brazil, but the problem was that it became hard in the
winter and soft and sticky in the summer. Charles Goodyear, an American, knew
there must be a solution. He tried many ways to make rubber a better material,
but he just lost money. Finally in 1839 he discovered that heat and sulfur made
weatherproof rubber. Unfortunately, he didn't apply for patents, and in 1843 an
Englishman, Thomas Hancock, reinvented "vulcanized" rubber and applied for a
patent a few weeks before Goodyear did! When Goodyear died in 1860, he was
$200,000 in debt. The Goodyear Tire and Rubber Company has nothing to do
with Charles Goodyear; it was just named in his honor.

Original inventor	What happened
What he invented	
Developed by	

c In pairs, discuss these questions.

1 What is one similarity between Elias Howe and Charles Goodyear?
2 What is one difference between them?
3 Why are patents important?
4 Why is Goodyear's name remembered but Howe's isn't?

3 Grammar builder: past passive

a Look at these examples and answer the questions.

Passive

*The sewing machine **was invented by** Elias Howe.*

*The company **was named** in Goodyear's honor.*

Active

*Elias Howe **invented** the sewing machine.*

*They **named** the company in Goodyear's honor.*

1 When do you think we use the passive voice rather than the active voice?
2 How is the past passive formed?
3 What does *by* indicate?
4 Is there a similar structure in your language?

b Change these sentences from active to passive voice.

1 Thomas Hancock patented vulcanized rubber in 1843.
2 Jonas Salk discovered the polio vaccine in 1957.
3 Robert Goddard launched the first liquid-fueled rocket in 1926.
4 The Swiss made the first milk chocolate bars in the 1870s.
5 Steve Jobs commercialized the Apple Macintosh computer in 1984.

4 Speaking and writing

Look at this example of a time capsule prepared by some Americans in 2000, to be opened in the year 3000. In groups, prepare a time capsule for your country. Include at least five objects.

Welcome to the past – The United States in the year 2000.

This is a picture of the White House, where the U.S. president lives. It was built in 1792.

These shoes were worn by Michael Jordan, a famous basketball player for the Chicago Bulls.

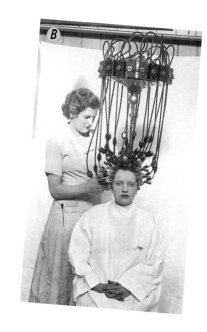

3 Different perspectives

1 Speaking

Look at the photographs of some early 20th century inventions. What do you think they were used for? Are similar things still used today?

2 Speaking and reading

a In pairs, discuss these questions.

1 What is this simple invention?

2 What is it used for?

3 What did people use before this product existed?

b Read the article quickly and number these events in order.

1 Mr. Fry discovers a use for the adhesive. ......

2 Development of the product stops. ......

3 The 3M company makes repositionable notes. ......

4 Mr. Silver invents an adhesive which is too weak. ......

c Now read the article again quickly and choose the best title.

1 Spencer Silver, Adhesives Expert

2 Invention or Discovery: The Story of Post-its®

3 3M Discovers Post-it® Notes

Stand out from the crowd

Discover the new Post-it Note colours and make your messages really stand out.

3M *Innovation*

Post-it Notes

There are many examples in history of things that were invented by mistake – things that were going to be one thing but became something else. For example, in 1970, a man named Spencer Silver, who worked for 3M, decided he was going to invent a new, stronger adhesive. He developed a new adhesive, but unfortunately, it was even weaker than the one 3M manufactured already. No one knew what to do with it, so work on the new adhesive was stopped.

One of Silver's colleagues, Arthur Fry, sang in a choir. Four years after Silver invented his adhesive, Fry remembered it and realized that there was a use for it. He used pieces of paper to find his place in his hymn book, but they kept falling out. He decided to use some of the adhesive to keep the paper in place. Because the adhesive was so weak, the paper could be removed and didn't damage the page.

Eventually, in 1980, ten years after Silver developed the very weak adhesive, 3M started selling Post-it® Notes, the repositionable notes that can easily be removed again. A great success story came from an unsuccessful beginning!

3 Grammar builder: *was / were going to*

a   Look at these examples.

Mr. Silver **was going to** *invent a stronger adhesive.*

We **were going to** *talk about famous inventions,* **but** *we talked about strange inventions instead.*

When do we use *was / were going to*?

a) for a situation in progress at a specific time in the past

b) for a future plan or intention

c) for a plan in the past which didn't happen

b   Complete the sentences in a logical way.

1   I was going to call you, but ...

2   We were going to invite you to the party, but ...

3   Chris was going to play tennis, but ...

4   They were going to move to Texas, but ...

4 Pronunciation: *weak forms – was / were*

a   Listen to the completed sentences from exercise 3b. Are your ideas similar?

b   Listen again. Notice the pronunciation of *was* and *were*. Are these words stressed?

c   In pairs, practice your sentences from exercise 3b.

5 Listening, writing and speaking

a   Listen to the conversation. What are they talking about?

b   Listen again. Then complete the sentences with information from the conversation.

1   Steve was going to go to ....,
    but he didn't because ....
    ....

2   Two years ago, he was going to ....,
    but he didn't because he ....
    ....

3   Last year, he ....
    He didn't because ....
    ....

c   In groups, talk about three things in your life that you were going to do but didn't do. Give reasons.

I was going to study veterinary medicine, but I wasn't good in math, so I studied languages.

4 Lifeline to I.T.

1 Speaking and reading

a In groups, discuss these questions.

1 What is the World Wide Web?   2 What do people use the Web for?   3 Do you use the Internet? If so, how?

b Read the text to find some of the answers to the questions.

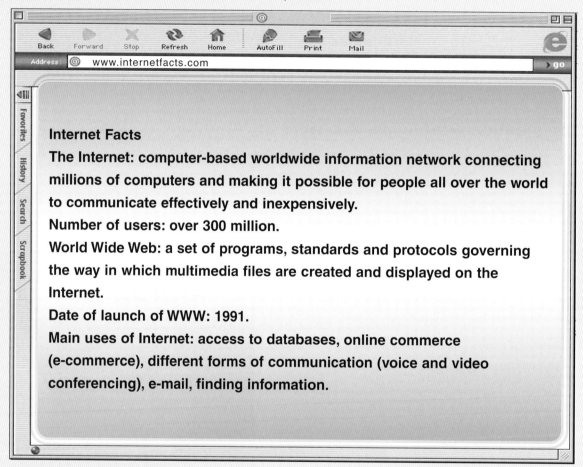

Address: www.internetfacts.com

Internet Facts

The Internet: computer-based worldwide information network connecting millions of computers and making it possible for people all over the world to communicate effectively and inexpensively.

Number of users: over 300 million.

World Wide Web: a set of programs, standards and protocols governing the way in which multimedia files are created and displayed on the Internet.

Date of launch of WWW: 1991.

Main uses of Internet: access to databases, online commerce (e-commerce), different forms of communication (voice and video conferencing), e-mail, finding information.

2 Listening

a Listen to the talk about Tim Berners-Lee. What did he do that is so remarkable?

b Listen again and number the events in the order you hear them.

1 He studied at Oxford. ......
2 He got a job at MIT (Massachusetts Institute of Technology). ......
3 He launched the World Wide Web. ......
4 He was born and raised in London. ......
5 He invented HTML (HyperText Mark-up Language). ......
6 He started to develop his ideas for the Web in Switzerland. ......

3 Speaking, reading and writing

a In pairs, look at the house in the photograph.

1 Does it look different from other houses?

2 What kind of house do you think it is?

b Read the article. Then in pairs, discuss these questions.

1 Where do you think the article comes from?

a) a scientific journal ......

b) an instruction manual ......

c) a general interest magazine ......

2 What are some of the problems mentioned in the article?

3 Do you think the article is a factual account?

Smart House

Nov. 28 – Moved in at last. Now we live in the smartest house in the neighborhood. Everything is networked. The cable TV is connected to the phone, which is connected to my personal computer. The computer is also connected to the electricity, the appliances and the security system.

Nov. 30 – Great! I programmed my VCR from the office, turned up the heating and switched on the lights with the car phone.

Dec. 3 – Yesterday the kitchen crashed! As I opened the refrigerator, the light bulb broke.

Immediately, everything else shut down – lights, microwave, coffee maker, everything. I called the cable company, who told me to call the electric company. They told me it's a software problem. The software company says it's an electrical problem.

Dec. 12 – Finally got the kitchen online, but now there's a virus in the house! I came home today and the living room is a sauna, the bedroom windows are covered with ice, the refrigerator has defrosted, the washing machine has flooded the laundry room and the TV is stuck on MTV! On my computer there is a

message: Welcome to the Home Destroyer Game!

Dec. 18 – The house is functioning now, but it's still a mess. The anti-virus team told me I was lucky – there's a worse virus than this!

Dec. 19 – We discover the house isn't insured for viruses. The insurance company is very sorry, but they can't anticipate every little problem.

Dec. 21 – The Smart House sales rep calls me. We can try the Smart House upgrade for free - our house can be even smarter! "Oh, great," I tell him.

c In groups, pick one room in your house and make it a "smart" room. Write a paragraph describing the room. Use ideas from the box to help you.

d Share your ideas with your classmates.

oven that makes food from recipes you program in

stereo that chooses music according to your mood

door that opens to let the dog in or out

windows that close when it rains

Unit 12 Consumerism

1 Patterns of buying

1 Speaking

a In pairs, look at the photographs. What are the most important factors for buying these kinds of items?

> price   quality   design
> convenience   other factors

b Make a list of the last three things you bought which weren't food. Why did you buy them? Compare your list with your partner.

2 Listening and speaking

a Listen to the conversation between two friends and check (✓) the articles of clothing you hear.

1 sneakers ○	5 blouse ○	9 T-shirt ○
2 sweater ○	6 jacket ○	10 top ○
3 jeans ○	7 dress ○	11 boots ○
4 skirt ○	8 shorts ○	12 shoes ○

b Listen to the conversation again. What do Stephanie and Ann each think about when they buy their clothes?

c In groups, answer these questions.

1 When was the last time you bought some clothes?

2 What did you buy?

3 Where did you buy them?

4 How long did you take to choose the clothes?

5 How did you pay for the clothes?

6 Why did you buy them?

3 Word builder: guessing meaning from context

a **Look at these sentences from exercise 2 and try to guess what the words in bold mean.**

1 Yes, but what's **fashionable** is important, too.

2 I bought an orange sweater because that's a **cool** color at the moment. Everybody's wearing orange.

3 If black's the **"in" color**, and you see it in all the magazines, you want to wear it.

4 If I had more money, I'd buy designer **stuff** but it's too expensive. So I usually look for **bargains**.

b **Answer the questions with your opinions.**

1 Name some fashionable trends.

2 What are the "in" colors this season?

3 What clothes do you think are cool?

4 Where can you usually find good bargains?

4 Reading and writing

a **Read the article quickly and identify the two types of promotion that are mentioned.**

Why do people buy certain products like make-up, perfume or even shampoo? Very often they decide what to buy based on what they see advertised in magazines or on TV. Cosmetics and other products are often endorsed by famous TV or movie stars or fashion models – people like Salma Hayek and Claudia Schiffer.

Lots of products are endorsed by famous people – particularly sports equipment. Soccer player Ronaldo endorses soccer equipment, tennis champion Pete Sampras promotes tennis rackets and golfer Tiger Woods endorses golf clubs. The idea is the same – if you use this type of tennis racket, you'll play tennis like Pete Sampras! Even movies are doing it – if you watch the James Bond movies closely, you'll see Omega wrist watches and Visa credit cards.

The other way companies promote their products is through sponsorship. Companies sponsor rock concerts, art exhibits and even big sports events like the Olympic Games. If you watch Formula 1 auto racing, you'll see lots of advertisements everywhere. Companies know that millions of

people watch these events and see their company's name. Does it work? Just ask yourself what brands of products you use.

b **Read the article again and answer these questions.**

1 What kinds of people endorse products?

2 Which sports are mentioned?

3 What kinds of events do companies sponsor?

4 Why do the two kinds of promotion mentioned work?

c **In groups, discuss these questions.**

1 What brands of products do you use?

2 Do you think advertising influenced your decision to buy them or was it a friend's influence?

3 In your country, who endorses products? Which companies sponsor events?

2 The hard sell

1 Speaking

a Which companies do you associate with these products? Write down one or two names for each product. Compare your answers with a partner.

> toothpaste   hamburgers   cola   jeans   computer programs
> video games   soap   car rental   sneakers

b Why do you think you remembered these companies?
How many of them are local and how many are international?

2 Reading and speaking

a Look at the pictures.

1 Where do you usually see advertisements?

2 What advertisements have you been seeing a lot recently?

3 What made you remember those particular advertisements?

b Now read the article and list the places where advertising is used.

ADVERTISING SELLS!

Years ago, companies discovered that advertising helped to sell more products and services. As early as the 1890s, advertising was already appearing everywhere – in newspapers and magazines, on billboards by the road, on the sides of buildings and even on paper bags. Companies also realized the importance of slogans to make their products more recognizable and memorable. Some slogans haven't changed: Heinz still has "57 Varieties," a slogan that Henry Heinz first used in 1896, even though he had more than 60 products at the time. The slogan was effective and Heinz has been using it since then.

Times haven't changed much. Advertisers have been using the same techniques for many years. They use people's anxieties about themselves to promote their products and make them buy books to improve their social skills, shampoo to stop dandruff and soaps that don't damage the skin. The names of products are also important – who doesn't know about Kellogg's Cornflakes and Big Macs? And what about trademarks – everybody knows these names: Marlboro, Coca-Cola, Intel, Budweiser, Pepsi, Gillette, Pampers, Nescafé and Bacardi. We know these things because we are bombarded on TV with advertisements for everything from cereal to cars 24 hours a day. And now? The Internet is the new place to advertise. It gives companies a new way of advertising that will probably change the way we shop.

c Read the text again and answer the questions.

1 Why do companies advertise their products or services?

2 Why do advertisers use slogans?

3 What is strange about the Heinz slogan?

4 What is one thing advertisers use to make people buy their products?

5 How may shopping change in the near future?

3 **Grammar builder:** present perfect vs. present perfect progressive

a **Look at these examples and answer the questions.**

Advertisers ***have been using*** *the same techniques for many years.*

The Internet ***has changed*** *the world of advertising.*

1 Which form is used to emphasize that an action is not over?

2 Which form is used for a finished action in the unspecified past?

a) present perfect

b) present perfect progressive

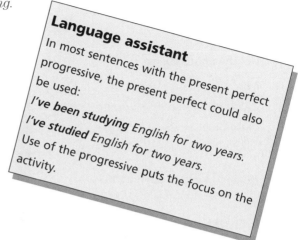

Language assistant

In most sentences with the present perfect progressive, the present perfect could also be used:

I've been studying English for two years.

I've studied English for two years.

Use of the progressive puts the focus on the activity.

b **Complete these sentences. Use the present perfect progressive when possible.**

1 Companies .... (*advertise*) on TV since the 1940s.

2 Many people .... (*start*) to buy products via the Internet.

3 Advertisers .... (*use*) slogans for over 100 years.

4 I'm tired because I .... (*study*) for an exam.

5 I .... (*finish*) writing my report.

4 **Listening, writing and speaking**

a **Listen to the interview with a marketing expert. List the four key factors she mentions for marketing a product or a service.**

b **In pairs, think of a new product or a new brand of product. Consider the four key factors. Then design an advertisement promoting your product.**

c **With another pair, discuss the advertisements and the marketing strategies. In your opinion:**

1 Has the other pair thought of a good product?

2 Have they been selling it at the correct price?

3 Have they been promoting it in the right places and in the right way?

4 Would their promotion convince you to buy the product? Why? / Why not?

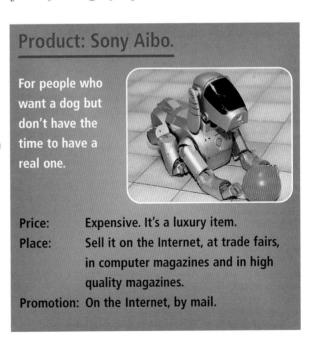

Product: Sony Aibo.

For people who want a dog but don't have the time to have a real one.

Price: Expensive. It's a luxury item.

Place: Sell it on the Internet, at trade fairs, in computer magazines and in high quality magazines.

Promotion: On the Internet, by mail.

3

Spotlight on a corporation

1 Speaking

Look at the photographs.

1 Who owns these products?
2 Which movies or TV programs have you seen made by this company?
3 Did you like them? Why? / Why not?

2 Word builder: collocation

You're going to read a text about Walt Disney. The text includes the following phrases.
Match the verbs with words to make the phrases.

1 win ...... 2 appear in ...... 3 set up ...... 4 invest ...... 5 work as ...... 6 employ ...... 7 launch ......

a) an advertising cartoonist   b) a studio   c) an Oscar   d) 750 artists

e) the first theme park   f) $1,499,000   g) the first sound cartoon

3 Reading, writing and speaking

a What do you know about Walt Disney?
Write three things you know about him or
his company and tell your classmates.

b In pairs, look at the fact sheets.

Student A, read the passage on page 113.
Ask student B questions to complete fact sheet A.
Student B, read the passage after the pronunciation
chart at the end of the book. Ask student A questions
to complete fact sheet B on page 109.

Walt Disney Fact Sheet A

Date of first full-length animated cartoon: ....

Amount of money Disney invested in it: ....

Amount of money it earned in two years: ....

Date and cost of Disneyland Park, California: ....

Location of other theme parks: ....

Date Disney died: ....

Walt Disney Fact Sheet B

Date Disney was born: ....

Place he was born: ....

His early interests: ....

His first job: ....

Date he went to Hollywood: ....

Date and place Mickey Mouse first appeared:

....

c Now read both texts to check your answers.
What other information did you learn about Walt Disney?

4 Pronunciation: review of numbers

a Read the rules. Then practice the numbers below.

a) With dates, use ordinal numbers. You see: *December 5, 1901.* You say: *December fifth, nineteen oh one.*

b) With money you see: *$8 million.* You say: *eight million dollars.*

c) Large numbers are divided into millions, thousands and hundreds: *1,377,468* is *one million, three hundred and seventy-seven thousand, four hundred and sixty-eight.*

1	January 27, 1989	3	270,860	5	$1,499,000
2	$4,240	4	March 4, 2001	6	8,934,756

b Listen and check.

c Write four numbers and dates. Read them to a partner and ask him/her to write them.
Check to see if they are correct.

5 Listening and speaking

a Work in groups and discuss the following. What activities is
The Walt Disney Company involved in? Which Disney products have you bought?

b Listen to the radio interview with a business journalist.
Check (✓) the business areas you hear for the Disney corporation.

TV and movie production ○   Cruise line ○

Theme parks ○   Agriculture ○

Fashion design ○   Internet companies ○

Publishing companies ○   Professional sports team franchises ○

Software company ○   ABC Television ○

c In groups, think of other big companies you know. What areas are they involved in?

Swatch, the watch maker, has now joined with Mercedes to make cars!

109

4 Lifeline to advertising and marketing

1 Listening and speaking

a In pairs, guess these facts about advertising.

General

1 In 2000, worldwide spending on advertising was
    a) $765.9 billion   **b)** $534.9 billion   **c)** $435.9 billion

2 Advertising spending in the U.S. last year grew by
    a) 2%   **b)** 7.1%   **c)** 10%

3 The most common form of advertising is
    a) radio   **b)** magazines   **c)** TV

Directed at children

1 The average American child watches .... TV advertisements per year.
    a) 10,000   **b)** 15,000   **c)** 20,000

2 Brand loyalty can begin to be established as early as age ....
    a) 2   **b)** 3   **c)** 4

3 Children age 14 and under spend .... per year of their own money (from allowances, gifts, etc.).
    a) $10 billion   **b)** $20 billion   **c)** $30 billion

---

b Listen to the first part of a talk on advertising and check your answers about general advertising.

c Listen to the second part of the talk and check your answers about children and advertising.

d What kinds of products are often advertised in your country? What are the most common forms of advertising?

2 Reading and speaking

a In pairs, discuss why you think advertisers focus so much on children.

b Read the article on page 111 quickly to find the answer to part a.

c Read the article again and mark the statements T (true) or F (false).

  1 Children spend $500 billion of their own money on products.   T ◯   F ◯

  2 Marketing of children's products used to focus on parents.   T ◯   F ◯

  3 A lot of advertising is now directed at children.   T ◯   F ◯

  4 Children can influence the products their parents buy.   T ◯   F ◯

  5 Different types of marketing are used to influence children.   T ◯   F ◯

Children's Purchasing Power

Today, children influence $500 billion worth of purchases every year, and as a result, marketing techniques have completely changed. In the past, the most effective way to sell children's products was through Mom and Dad.

Now the opposite is true: children are the object of intense advertising pressure by companies seeking to influence billions of dollars in family spending.

Advertisers are aware that children influence the purchase not just of kids' products, but everything in the household from cars to toothpaste. Consequently, these "adult" products are being combined with child-oriented logos and images. Different marketing tools have spread into children's lives – examples are kid versions of adult magazines, promotional toys linked to movies or TV shows and logos on all kinds of merchandise everywhere children go.

3 Word builder: synonyms

Match these words from the text with their meanings.

1	purchases	a)	looking
2	techniques	b)	instruments
3	products	c)	consumer goods
4	seeking	d)	connected with
5	household	e)	home
6	tools	f)	things you buy
7	linked to	g)	methods

4 Writing and speaking

a In pairs, think of an advertisement aimed at children.
Use the questions in the box and the example below to help write a description.

> What kind of advertisement is it? TV, radio, billboard, etc.
>
> Which product is it advertising?
>
> How often does this advertisement appear?
>
> Which children is it aimed at? Girls, boys or both?
>
> Is it aimed at very young children?
>
> Do you think the advertisement is effective? Why or why not?

This is a TV advertisement for video games. It's on TV every afternoon / during all the children's programs. It's mostly aimed at boys aged 10 to 13. We think it's very effective because the boys in the advertisement look like they're having a great time, and the video games are promoted as the latest "in" thing. You aren't "cool" if you don't have them.

b Now describe the advertisement to another pair.

Checkpoint 6

1 Check your progress

a Complete this e-mail with one word in each space.

Arial 12 B / U

Hi, Helga

How are things in Vienna? Sorry I (1)..................... written for a long time. It
has (2)..................... raining here in Rio (3)..................... last weekend. I was
(4)..................... to write you yesterday, (5)..................... my Internet connection
(6)..................... not working. Anyway, I'm on–line again now.
What's new? Well, the big thing is that I (7)..................... graduated at last!
Yes, I'm a chemical engineer — it's official! The degree certificates
(8)..................... presented (9)..................... the Education Secretary, and the
ceremony (10)..................... reported in all the main newspapers.
Well, Helga, that's all for now. Write asnd tell me what you have been doing.

Best wishes, João

---

b Complete the second sentence so that it means the same as the first.

11 They say Renoir painted this picture.

They say this picture ....

12 We were driven to the airport by my brother.

My brother .... to the airport.

13 I visited France in 1997 and 1999.

I .... twice, and I hope to go there again.

14 We started working ten hours ago, and we have to work another two hours.

We have ...., and we have to work another two hours.

15 The idea was to take the early bus, but we missed it.

We .... the early bus, but we missed it.

Score out of 20

○ 18–20 Excellent! ○ 15–17 Very good! ○ 12–14 OK, but review. ○ 9–11 You have some problems. Review units 11 and 12. ○ 0–8 Talk to your teacher.

112

2 Games to play

As a class or in groups of five or more, follow these instructions.

1 Form a closed circle or square.

2 Take a clean sheet of paper and write this at the top:
   Jane Pond, secret agent 008, left the hotel at
   6 o'clock that summer morning in Paris. She ...

3 Complete the second sentence of the story.

4 Pass your sheet of paper to the student on your left, and take the paper from the student on your right.

5 Write a third sentence on the other student's paper.

6 Continue passing the papers and adding a sentence until you get your own paper back.

7 Write one or two final sentences on your paper.

8 Stick your paper on the board or wall.

9 Read all the stories, and vote for the best one.

3 My world

a How will you continue to improve your English? Mark the activities with a check (✓) if you plan to do it, or a cross (✗) if you don't.

b In groups, discuss your plans. Say why you will do some things and why you won't do others.

4 Personal word bank

a Write a list of ten English words that your classmates might not know.

b In pairs, look at each other's lists of words. Are there any you don't know? Ask your partner to explain them.

c If you have doubts or disagreements, check the words in a dictionary.

Unit 12 Lesson 3 exercise 3 student A

Walt Disney was born in Chicago on December 5, 1901. He became interested in drawing and photography at an early age. After the First World War, he worked as an advertising cartoonist in Kansas City and created his first animated cartoon. In 1923 he went to Hollywood where his brother was living. He arrived there with only $40 in his pocket. Walt and his brother borrowed $500 and set up a studio to produce animated cartoons. Mickey Mouse was created in 1928 and appeared in the first sound cartoon, *Steamboat Willie*.

1 Study with a teach-yourself English course.

2 Listen to music in English.

3 Read magazines and books in English.

4 Get an English-speaking boyfriend / girlfriend or husband / wife.

5 Take another English course.

6 Spend some time in an English-speaking country.

7 Write to a pen-pal in another country.

8 "Chat" with people in other countries on the Internet.

9 Look for foreigners in your city to talk to in English.

10 Other: ....

Songsheet 1
Trains and boats and planes

1 Speaking

a Put the pictures in the correct order.

b Now invent a story about the pictures.

A   B   C   D

....

2 Listening

a Listen to the song. Match the verses with the pictures.

Trains and boats and planes

1 Trains and boats and planes are passing by
They mean a trip to Paris or Rome
To someone else but not for me
The trains and the boats and planes
Took you away, away from me

2 We were so in love and high above
We had a star to wish upon.
Wish and dreams come true, but not for me
The trains and the boats and planes
Took you away, away from me

3 You are from another part of the world
You had to go back a while and then
You said you soon would return again
I'm waiting here like I promised to
I'm waiting here but where are you

4 Trains and boats and planes took you away
But every time I see them I pray
And if my prayer can cross the sea
The trains and the boats and planes
Will bring you back, back home to me.

b Listen again. Mark these sentences T (true) or F (false).

1 The woman isn't traveling anywhere.   T ◯   F ◯

2 She loved the man but he didn't love her.   T ◯   F ◯

3 He was from another country.   T ◯   F ◯

4 He went away and promised he would come back.   T ◯   F ◯

5 She is waiting for him to come back.   T ◯   F ◯

3 Reading and writing

a Read this letter from the woman in the song.

How is she feeling?   **a)** confident   **b)** angry   **c)** confused

Dear Daniel,
I went to the sea today and looked for you but you weren't there.
When are you coming back?
You said you would be back soon and I'm waiting for you.
I haven't heard from you for a long time – what's happening?
Please write to me.
I miss you.

Love,

Anna

b Imagine you are Daniel. Answer the letter. Use the questions in the box to help you.

Are you coming back?

If so, when are you coming back?

If not, why not?

Dear Anna,

I'm sorry I haven't written for a long time but ...

Songsheet 2
If you don't know me by now

1 Word builder: relationships

a **Match the phrases with their meanings.**

1 To break up   a) To have a romance

2 To get yourself together   b) To believe that you can depend on someone

3 To be funny   c) To finish, especially a relationship

4 To see eye to eye   d) To agree

5 To trust in someone   e) To be strange

6 To have a love affair   f) To organize yourself

b **Now complete the sentences using phrases from part a. You may need to change the form of the verb.**

Jane is really depressed because ..*she broke up*. with Carl.

1 Don't put Liz next to Jake at dinner – they don't ....

2 You're not working very hard this term Maria – you'll have to ....

if you want to pass the exam.

3 That .... I've seen that boy three times today!

4 You can definitely .... me – I won't hurt you.

5 They .... a few years ago – now they're both happily married.

6 They .... last week – they had a big argument.

2 Listening

Listen to the song and answer these questions.

1 Who is the singer?

   a) the woman's brother   **b)** the woman's ex-husband   **c)** the woman's lover

2 What is the singer's message?

   a) We don't understand each other so we should break up.

   b) We have to trust each other to make this relationship work.

   c) The relationship is OK, but you are jealous sometimes.

If you don't know me by now

If you don't know me by now
You will never, never, never know me

All the things that we've been through
You should understand me like I understand you
Now, girl, I know the difference between right and wrong
I ain't gonna do nothing to break up our happy home
Don't get so excited when I come home a little late at night
'Cos we only act like children when we argue, fuss and fight

If you don't know me by now
You will never, never, never know me

We've all got our own funny moods
I've got mine, woman, you've got yours too
Just trust in me like I trust in you
As long as we've been together, it should be so easy to do
Just get yourself together or we might as well say goodbye
What good is a love affair when you can't see eye to eye?

If you don't know me by now
You will never, never, never know me

3 Speaking and writing

a In pairs, discuss this question.

What are the most important ingredients in a good relationship?

It is important to respect each other.

b In groups, make a list of six of the most important things for a successful relationship.

Songsheet 3
Every breath you take

1 Word builder: meanings

Match the words or expressions with their meanings.

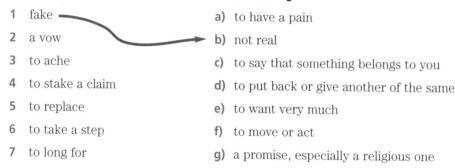

1   fake   a) to have a pain
2   a vow   b) not real
3   to ache   c) to say that something belongs to you
4   to stake a claim d) to put back or give another of the same
5   to replace   e) to want very much
6   to take a step   f) to move or act
7   to long for   g) a promise, especially a religious one

2 Pronunciation: sounds – "a" and "e"

a   Match the words with the sounds. There are two words for each sound.

1 fake   2 day   3 see   4 repl**ace**   5 aches   6 face   7 me   8 play

a) /eɪ/   b) /eɪk/   c) /i/   d) /eɪs/

b   In pairs, put these words in the appropriate column according to their sound.

make   stay   take   break   say   trace   stake   embrace   be

/eɪk/	/eɪ/	/i/	/eɪs/

3 Listening

a   Listen to the song. How is the singer feeling?

a) happy   b) sad   c) bored

b   Complete the song with words from exercise 2.

Every breath you take

Every breath you .....take.....

Every move you (1) ....

Every bond you (2) ....

Every step you (3) ....

I'll be watching you.

Every single ......day......

Every word you (4) ....

Every game you (5) ....

Every night you (6) ....

I'll be watching you.

Oh can't you (7) ....

You belong to (8) ....

How my poor heart (9) ....

With every step you (10) ....

Every move you (11) ....

Every vow you (12) ....

Every smile you (13) ....

Every claim you (14) ....

I'll be watching you.

Since you've been gone I've been lost without a (15) ....

I dream at night I can only see your (16) ....

I look around but it's you I can't (17) ....

I feel so cold and I long for your (18) ....

I keep crying, baby, baby, please ...

b **Listen again and check your answers.**

4 Speaking

a **In pairs, discuss these questions.**

1 Do you think the singer is an obsessed fan, an ex-boyfriend or a jealous husband?

2 Why do you think he's watching her?

b **Give reasons for your answers.**

He's watching her because he's missing her.

Songsheet 4
Eternal flame

1 Word builder: parts of the body

a Label the parts of the body.

b Add more labels.

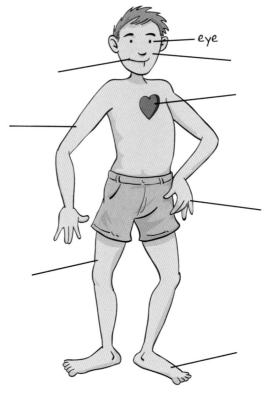

eye

2 Listening

a Before you listen, use the pictures to guess what the missing words are.

Eternal flame

Close your (1) 👁️ ...., give me your (2) 🤚 . ..., darling

Do you feel my (3) 🖤 .... beating?

Do you understand?

Do you feel the same?

Am I only (4) 💭 ....?

Is this burning an eternal (5) 🔥 ....?

I believe it's meant to be, darling

I want you when you are (6) 😴.....................

You belong with me

Do you feel the same?

Am I only (7) 💭 ....?

Is this burning an eternal (8) 🔥 ....?

Say my name, (9) ☀️ .... shines through the (10) 🌧️ ....

A whole life, so lonely

And then come and ease the pain

I don't want to lose this feeling.

b Now listen to the song and check your answers.

c What does the singer mean when she asks "Is this burning an eternal flame?"?

3 Pronunciation: different sounds

a Say the words and notice the different sounds.

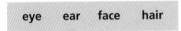

| eye | ear | face | hair |

b Now put these words in the correct column according to the sound.

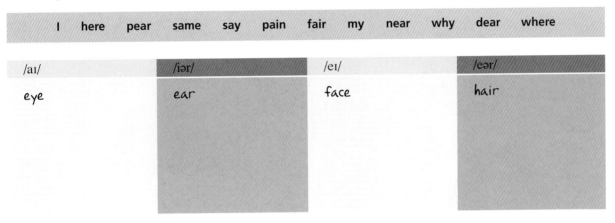

| I | here | pear | same | say | pain | fair | my | near | why | dear | where |

/aɪ/	/iər/	/eɪ/	/eər/
eye	ear	face	hair

c In pairs, repeat the words. Can you add any more?

4 Speaking

a Match the pictures with the commands.

1 Bend your knees and close your eyes.

2 Touch your nose.

3 Stand on one leg.

B

A

C

b Now listen to your teacher and play the game *Simon Says*.

Songsheet 5
Change

1 Writing

Complete the sentences about yourself.

If I could change my hair, _I'd have long black curly hair._ ....

1   If I could change my nationality, ...

2   If I could change my house, ...

3   If I could change my name, ...

4   If I could change the way I live my life today, ...

5   If I could change ....

2 Listening

Listen to the song and answer the questions.

1   Is the singer

    a) happy with her life?   **b)** unhappy with her life?

2   Is the singer

    a) looking for a boyfriend?   **b)** in love?

3   Does the singer want to

    a) reassure the person she is singing to?   **b)** frighten them?   **c)** make them laugh?

Change

If I could change the way I live my life today, I wouldn't change a single thing,
'Cos if I changed my world into another place, I wouldn't see your smiling face.

Honey, don't you worry, there's nothin' to worry for:
'Cos if I didn't love you, I wouldn't be here now
And if I didn't want you, I would have turned around by now.

You've got to believe me, babe, believe that I love you so,
'Cos if I didn't love you, I would have turned around
And if I didn't want you, I would want you out.

This love, this love has filled me up.
Ooh my love, I'll never give you up
'Cos I'll always want your love.

If I could change the way I live my life today,
I wouldn't change a single thing
'Cos if I changed my world into another place
I wouldn't see your smiling face.

Believing is the answer, the answer to all your fears.
When I first said I loved you, I went in for the kill.
Now when I say I love you, I mean I always will.

This love, this love has filled me up.
Ooh my love, I'll never give you up
'Cos I'll always want your love.

3 Writing and speaking

a **Answer the questions about yourself.**

1 What would you do if you were president of your country?

....

2 What job would you do if you could do anything?

....

3 If you could get married to anyone in the world, who would you marry?

....

b **Write two more questions to ask your group.**

....

....

c **Now in groups, ask and answer your questions.**

Songsheet 6
Lean on me

1 Word builder: definitions

Match the phrases with the definitions.

1 I'm right up the road.

2 Call on me.

3 Do you need a hand?

4 Lean on me.

5 Swallow your pride.

a) Can I help you?

b) I live near you.

c) Visit me (or ask me for help).

d) Don't be afraid to ask for help.

e) Let me support you (physically / emotionally).

2 Word builder: synonyms

a Match the words or phrases which mean the same.

1 sorrow

2 wise

3 to carry

4 to carry on

5 load

a) smart

b) to bear

c) to continue

d) heavy thing

e) sadness

b These are all important words or ideas from the song. What do you think the song is about?

a) friendship   b) unhappy love   c) work

3 Listening

a Listen to the song and check the answer to exercise 2b.

b Circle the correct verb form.

I'll *be* / *to be* your friend.

1 It *won't be* / *to be* long.

2 … if I have things you need *borrow* / *to borrow*.

3 I need somebody *lean* / *to lean on*.

4 I might *have* / *to have* a problem.

c Listen again and check your answers.

Lean on me

Sometimes in our lives we all have pain
We all have sorrow
But if we are wise
We know that there's always tomorrow

Lean on me, when you're not strong
And I'll be your friend
I'll help you carry on
For it won't be long
'Til I'm gonna need somebody to lean on

Please swallow your pride
If I have faith you need to borrow
For no one can fill those of your needs
That you won't let show

You just call on me, brother, when you need a hand
We all need somebody to lean on
I just might have a problem that you'll understand
We all need somebody to lean on

Lean on me, when you're not strong
And I'll be your friend
I'll help you carry on
For it won't be long
'Til I'm gonna need somebody to lean on

You just call on me, brother, when you need a hand
We all need somebody to lean on
I just might have a problem that you'll understand
We all need somebody to lean on

If there is a load you have to bear
That you can't carry
I'm right up the road
I'll share your load
If you just call me

d   What is the significance of the title _Lean on me_?

4 Speaking

In pairs, discuss the questions.

1   What are friends for? (e.g. going
    out with / talking to about problems /
    having fun with)

2   "We all need somebody to lean on."
    Do you agree?

3   Are friends more important to you
    than family?

4   Who do _you_ call on when you have
    a problem?

Irregular verbs

Infinitive	Past simple	Past participle	Unit and Lesson
be	was / were	been	U1, L1
beat	beat	beaten	U8, L1
become	became	become	U6, L3
begin	began	begun	Checkpoint 2
blow	blew	blown	U3, L1
break	broke	broken	U2, L1
bring	brought	brought	U4, L4
buy	bought	bought	U1, L3
catch	caught	caught	U5, L1
choose	chose	chosen	U2, L1
come	came	come	U4, L1
cost	cost	cost	U1, L3
cut	cut	cut	U4, L4
drink	drank	drunk	U3, L4
drive	drove	driven	U1, L3
eat	ate	eaten	U3, L3
fall	fell	fallen	U9, L4
feed	fed	fed	U8, L4
feel	felt	felt	U1, L2
find	found	found	Checkpoint 2
fly	flew	flown	U10, L2
get	got	gotten	Checkpoint 1
give	gave	given	U4, L2
go	went	gone / been	U1, L2
grow	grew	grown	U4, L4
have	had	had	U1, L1
keep	kept	kept	U9, L3
know	knew	known	U6, L2
let	let	let	U9, L1
lie	lay	lain	U10, L1
lose	lost	lost	U3, L3

Infinitive	Past simple	Past participle	Unit and Lesson
make	made	made	U4, L2
meet	met	met	U9, L3
pay	paid	paid	U5, L3
put	put	put	U7, L2
ride	rode	ridden	U1, L3
rise	rose	risen	U8, L2
run	ran	run	U3, L4
say	said	said	U10, L2
see	saw	seen	U4, L1
sell	sold	sold	U5, L3
set	set	set	U12, L3
shake	shook	shaken	U1, L2
shine	shone	shone	U3, L1
shut	shut	shut	U11, L4
sing	sang	sung	Checkpoint 3
sit	sat	sat	U4, L2
sleep	slept	slept	U1, L2
speak	spoke	spoken	Checkpoint 3
spend	spent	spent	U1, L3
split	split	split	U3, L1
spread	spread	spread	U4, L4
stand	stood	stood	U4, L2
stick	stuck	stuck	Checkpoint 6
take	took	taken	U2, L1
teach	taught	taught	U10, L3
tell	told	told	U5, L2
think	thought	thought	U1, L2
throw	threw	thrown	U7, L1
wear	wore	worn	U7, L1
win	won	won	U5, L1
write	wrote	written	U9, L3

Pronunciation chart

Vowels

/i/	eat
/ɪ/	sit
/eɪ/	wait
/e/	get
/æ/	hat
/aɪ/	write
/ʌ/	but
/uː/	food
/ʊ/	good
/oʊ/	go
/ɔː/	saw
/a/	hot
/aʊ/	cow
/ɔɪ/	boy
/iər/	here
/ər/	her
/eər/	hair
/or/	or
/ar/	far

Consonants
(shown as initial sounds)

/b/	bat
/k/	cat
/tʃ/	chair
/d/	dog
/f/	fat
/g/	girl
/h/	hat
/dʒ/	July
/l/	like
/m/	man
/n/	new
/p/	pet
/kw/	queen
/r/	run
/s/	see
/ʃ/	shirt
/t/	talk
/ð/	the
/θ/	thin
/v/	voice
/w/	where
/j/	you
/ŋ/	sing (as final sound)
/z/	zoo

The alphabet

/eɪ/	/i/	/e/	/aɪ/	/oʊ/	/uː/	/ar/
Aa	Bb	Ff	Ii	Oo	Qq	Rr
Hh	Cc	Ll	Yy		Uu	
Jj	Dd	Mm			Ww	
Kk	Ee	Nn				
	Gg	Ss				
	Pp	Xx				
	Tt					
	Vv					
	Zz					

Unit 12 Lesson 3 exercise 3 student B

In 1937, Disney produced the first full-length animated musical cartoon, *Snow White and the Seven Dwarfs*. Walt invested the huge sum of $1,499,000 and employed 750 artists to do the animation. It was a massive hit and earned $8 million in two years. It was followed by other full-length animated classics such as *Pinocchio, Fantasia, Dumbo* and *Bambi*.
In 1955, he launched Disneyland Park in California at a cost of $17 million. By 1985, 250 million people had visited the theme park. There are now theme parks in Orlando, Paris and Tokyo. During his career, Disney won 32 Oscars for his movies. He died in 1966 and was one of the greatest influences in the world of entertainment.

Macmillan Publishers Limited
Companies and representatives throughout the world

ISBN 978 0 333 92681 9

Text © Simon Brewster, Paul Davies, Mickey Rogers 2001
Songsheets written by Kate Fuscoe

Design and illustration © Macmillan Publishers Limited 2001

First published 2001

All rights reserved; no part of this publication may be reproduced, stored in a retrieval system, transmitted in any form, or by any means, electronic, mechanical, photocopying, recording, or otherwise, without the prior written permission of the publishers.

Designed by Oliver Hickey, based on original design by Kevin Mcgeoghegan

Illustrated by Martin Ashton, Red Giraffe, Rob Loxton, Sue Potter, Gavin Reece, Paul Scholfield, Andy Warrington, Geoff Waterhouse.

Cover photograph by Stone

The publishers would like to thank the following for reading the material and making comments: María Inês Albernaz, English Teacher, Centro Federal de Educação Tecnológica, CEFET-Campos, Brazil and English Teacher, Instituto Brasil, Estados Unidos de Campos, Brazil; Florinda Scremin Marquez, ELT/ESP Professor and Coordinator, FESP, Curitiba, Brazil; Vládia María Cabral Borges, Professor of English Linguistics and Applied Linguistics, Head of Department of Foreign Languages, University of Ceará, Forteleza, Brazil; Monica Myers, English in Action, São Paulo, Brazil; Luís Manuel Malta de Alves Louceiro, Coordinator, ESL Institute, English at Sabin, São Paulo, Brazil; Ricardo Romero-Medina, Associate Professor, Foreign Languages Department, Universidad Nacional de Colombia, Bogotá, Colombia; Clara Inês García, Head of Language Center, Universidad Militar Nueva Granada, Bogotá; María Teresa Barrera Castillo, Department of Languages, Universidad Veracruzana, Mexico; Alina Blanco, UPEAP University, Puebla, Mexico; Jean-Pierre Brossard, Academic Director, Proulex, Guadalajara, Mexico; Teresa Castineira, English Teacher, Benemérita Universidad Autónoma de Puebla, Mexico; Adriana Lucía Patricia Dorantes González, Head of Languages Department, Universidad Autónoma Agraria, Saltillo, Mexico; Albina Escobar, Freelance Teacher Trainer and Consultant, Mexico; Norma Duarte Martinez, English Coordinator, Veterinary Medicine and Husbandry College, Universidad Nacional Autónoma de México, Coyoacan, Mexico; Carol Lethaby, ELT Teacher Trainer/Consultant, Department of Modern Languages, Universidad de Guadalajara/The British Council, Mexico; Connie Rae Johnson, Professor and Teacher, Universidad de las Américas, Puebla, Mexico; Vera Lucía Lovato Bruno, Director and Teacher, Vertex Express English Course, Brazil.

The publishers gratefully acknowledge the following for permission to reproduce copyright material: Extract from A Brief History of Time by Stephen Hawking, published by Bantam Press, a division of Transworld Publishers. © Space Time Publications Limited 1988. All Rights Reserved. Reprinted with permission of Transworld Publishers; Extract about Stephen Hawking reprinted by arrangement with Writers House LLC, as agent for Stephen Hawking; Extracts one color slide depicting various licensed DISNEY T-shirts, one color slide depicting Sleeping Beauty Castle at DISNEYLAND ® Park, one color disc image depicting the videocassettte tape cover of Walt Disney Home Video WALT DISNEY CHRISTMAS, one black and white photograph depicting Mr. Walt Disney, and one color slide from Walt Disney's animated feature SNOW WHITE AND THE SEVEN DWARFS © Disney Enterprises Inc. Reprinted with the kind permission of Walt Disney Enterprises, Inc.; Extract from Notes from a Small Island by Bill Bryson published by Doubleday, a division of Transworld Publishers © Bill Bryson 1995. All Rights Reserved. Reprinted with permission of Transworld Publishers; Heinz logo reprinted with permission of H.J. Heinz Company; Extract from Madame Tussaud's brochure reprinted with permission of Madame Tussaud's; Extract about McDonald's and logo reprinted with permission of McDonald's; Extract from World's Biggest Cities adapted from Newsweek 10th June, 1996. © 1996 Newsweek Inc. All Rights Reserved. Used with permission; Extract Smart House by Michael Schrage. Reprinted with permission of the author; Extract about Sony Aibo reprinted with permission of Sony United Kingdom Limited; Extract about 3M Post-It ® notes and Post-It ® notes advertisement, reprinted with permission of 3M; Science Trivia Quiz: extract from tomorrowtoday.com reprinted with permission of TomorrowToday.com; Extract about Ben and Jerry's reprinted with permission of Unilever Press Office; Netscape screenshot © 2001 Netscape Communications Corporation. Used with permission; Trains and Boats and Planes words by Hal David, Music by Burt Bacharach © 1964 New Hidden Valley Music and Casa David Music, USA. Warner/Chappell Music Ltd, London, W6 8BS. Reproduced by permission of International Music Publications Ltd. All Rights Reserved.; If You Don't Know Me By Now words and music by Leon Huff and Kenneth Gamble © 1990 Warner-Tamerlane Publishing Corp, USA. Warner/Chappell Music Ltd, London, W6 8BS. Reproduced by permission of International Music Publications Ltd. All Rights Reserved.; Every Breath You Take words and music by Sting © 1983. Reproduced by permission of EMI Music Publishing Ltd/Magnetic Publishing Ltd, London, WC2H 0QY; Eternal Flame written by Steinberg, Kelly & Huffs (Sony/ATV Tunes Publishing LLC), reprinted by permission of Sony ATV Music Publishing (UK) Ltd.; Change written by Stansfield/Devaney/Morris (Big Life Music Ltd), reprinted by permission of the publisher; Lean On Me words and music by Bill Withers © 1972 Interior Music Inc, USA. Reproduced by permission of EMI Music Publishing Ltd, London WC2H 0QY.
Every effort has been made to trace copyright holders, but in some cases this has proved impossible. The publishers would be happy to hear from any copyright holder that has not been acknowledged.

Picture research by Penni Bickle

Commissioned photographs by Yiorgos Nikiteas pp18(d), 42, 48(CDs), 62(A,C), 64(l), 96(B,C,D), 98(pills,gum), 104(stereo, trainers), 106(products), 111, 119

The authors and publishers would like to thank the following for permission to reproduce their photographs:
©3M p100(bl); Allsport p96(A), 105(Tiger Woods); BBC p21(lion – P Blackwell); Private Collection/Ken Walsh/Mary Wollstonecraft Shelley(1797-1851) (engraving) by Richard Rothwell (1800-86) (after)Bridgeman Art Library p82(tl); Corbis pp11(r – Jacobs Stock Photography), 78(A), 79; The Culture Archive p100(crank), 106(candy); James Davis p36(l), 46/7, 52, 86(t,b), 92(C,F); ©The Walt Disney Corporation pp108, 109 ; Greg Evans p27(b); Mary Evans p33(L'Illustration); Eye Ubiquitous pp20(b), 24(r), 48(gas pump), 49, 50, 61(r), 64(r), 78(C), 86(b), 91, 98(CD), 104(CDs); Hulton Getty pp78(B), 88(old bus), 92(B), 100(B); Ronald Grant Cinema Archive p82(tr,br); London Aerial Photo Library p81; Magnum pp36(r - Marlow), 44(b – S Meiselas), 53(Gruaert), 56/7(McCurry), 60(Harvey – Day of the Dead), 66(B – Steele Perkins), 92(A – Mayar), 97(Burri); PBR p43; Pictor pp16, 17(bl), 45, 117, 123, 124, 125; Retna pp6(tr – Melia), 9(G Minsdale), 18(a,b,c,e,f), 19(G Hinsdale), 20(a,background), 22(A Gallo), 27(t) 104(perfume, jeans, watch) - J Acheson), 28(bl), 32(Statue of Liberty - A Carruth), 54(r – Photofest), 60(B – P Reeson), 62(B – R Dankloff), 70(tl – Calvert/Sunshine, br – J Acheson), 78(D – D Atlas), 80(Black), 84(B Talesnick), 92(D), 101(K Kochey), 105(C. Schiffer – T. Wood); Rex Features pp6(tl,b – Rooke), 10(Larkins), 18(c), 65, 82(bl), 107(Kyriacou); Science Photo Library pp8(t – E H RAO), 26(B – P Menzel, C – Laguna Design), 27(D – TEK Image), 28(Adam Hart Davis, Dr Ray Clark), 40(Tom Van Sant), 68(head – Tomkinson), 68/9(background – Pasieka), 74, 84(background – Royal Observatory), 100(A – Science Museum), 102(H Morhan); David Simson pp8(b), 13, 28(br), 32(l), 34, 48(bus), 60(C,D,E), 61(c), 66(A), 75, 88(fast train, passengers), 88/9(background), 92(E), 96(E), 106(Coca-Cola); Stone p11(l); Telegraph Colour Library pp44(t), 60(A), 69, 98(tyres), 99(White House); Trip & Art Directors pp17(br), 31, 35, 46/7, 48(car, movie theatre), 61(l), 73; View p103(J Millar); Zul pp21(background), 24(l – T Freeman), 32/3, 48(bread), 50, 62(D,E), 63, 88(plane), 98(microwave, bike, sewing machine)

The publishers would like to thank the Mosaic Restaurant, Brighton, and EF International School of English, Brighton.

Among all the people who contributed to the Skyline project, the authors give special thanks to John Waterman and Manuela Lima, who did much more than their duty as editors. Thank you, John and Manuela! The authors would also like to thank Katie Austin for the cover designs.

Printed in Thailand

2012 2011 2010 2009 2008
17   16   15   14   13